THE CASPIAN

By

BRENDA DALTON

British Library Cataloguing in Publication Data

A Catalogue Record for this book is available from the British Library

ISBN 0-9549362-2-1

First published 1999 by
HORSESHOE PUBLICATIONS
Box 37, Kingsley, Warrington,
Cheshire, WA6 8DR

Front cover:
Chippendale Bahram — Caspian stallion
Texas, USA
Photo Credit: Dru Harper

Back cover:
The Author with foundation mare Shirine* (right)
Photo Credit: The Ormskirk Advertiser

Printed in Great Britain by
Plausible Publishing Limited
Yetminster, Dorset

The story of the discovery of the Caspian Pony by Louise Firouz
in northern Iran in 1965, and her subsequent valiant struggles
against every sort of obstacle to build up a viable breeding
group, makes fascinating reading. Brenda Dalton, who put together
the International Caspian Pony Stud Book, is just the person to
write it.

My part in the story is very simple. I think it was during a
visit to Iran for the 1,500th anniversary of the Persian monarchy,
that I attended a display of Iranian horses and ponies organised
by the then Royal Horse Society. Louise Firouz was present and
showed some of her ponies. She told me the story of her discovery
and of her attempt to re-establish the breed. During the course of
the conversation it occurred to me that the whole scheme would be
at serous risk if any disease, or other misfortune was to hit her
small stud and so I suggested that it might be an idea to move a
few breeding animals to another location. I offered to look after
any ponies which she might care to send to Britain. She accepted
the idea and in due course, and after every sort of quarantine
vicissitude, which involved two years in Hungary, the stallion
Rostam and the mares Momtaz-e-Mahal and Khorshid Kola together
with Atesheh, the daughter of Rostam and Khorshid Kola (born whilst
they were in Hungary) arrived safely in this country.

As events in Iran unfolded over the next 30 years, this movement
of breeding stock proved its worth and its descendents now form
the greater part of the breed outside Iran.

ACKNOWLEDGEMENTS

I would like to thank my family and friends, who have supported my involvement with Caspian horses for the last twenty five years, and Shirine*, a very special Caspian horse.

Also:

H.R.H. Prince Philip
Louise Firouz
Elizabeth Alderson
Lawrence Alderson
E. Gus Cothran
Paul Gradwell
Jane Scott
National Registrars
Caspian owners and breeders
Colleagues at Tarleton High School, Lancashire

෨෬

Special thanks go to the following, without whose help this book may not have been published:

Joyce Covington
Julie Hooi
Vicki Hudgins
John Schneider-Merck
Jane & Ron Scott
Les & Anne Stevens
Shahram Dordari

All line drawings were produced by Lez Harvey

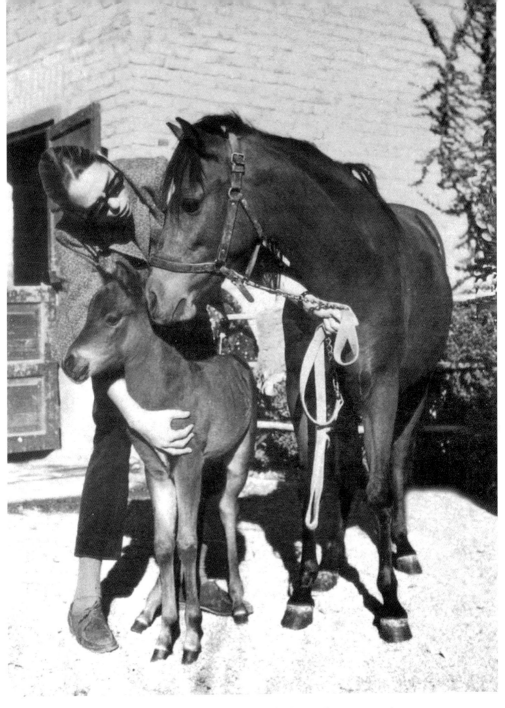

Louise Firouz with Momtaz-e-Mahal who was later presented to
HRH Prince Philip

Yearling colts bred by ProtoArabian in the USA - 1997

Chippendale Bahram - Caspian stallion bred in Australia and exported to the USA
(photo: Dru Harper)

CONTENTS

Louise and Narcy Firouz
Louise Firouz rediscovered the Caspian horse in 1965 on the
southern shores of the Caspian Sea in Northern Iran

A breed of tiny horses drew chariots which carried King Darius, hunting lions, on an ancient Persian seal, some 2500 years ago. Through some strange fluke, they survived to the latter part of the 20th century. Historical neglect probably saved them. Since no-one appears to have paid them any attention in the last 1000 years they have neither been 'improved' nor segregated. They have survived in herds, roaming semi-wild in the Alborz mountains of northern Iran and along the Caspian coast. Recent attempts to collect and preserve the pitifully few specimens left have shown how easy it is to destroy a whole sub-species of animal by removing them to one place.

What saved it, in Iran, was its own obscurity. While specimens were collected and bred on one farm, nationalized, and then destroyed as a side-effect of revolution, it managed to survive in its neglected semi-wild state. It was not bred for particular characteristics and, in its own land, apart from my family, only a handful of veterinarians appreciated the value of this anachronistic horse. A dedicated group of people, led by HRH Prince Philip, saved the Caspian outside Iran. Had it not been for the British, the Caspian would have passed quietly into oblivion soon after it was 'rediscovered' in 1965.

This is the story of the Caspian as we know it and as we have reconstructed it. It provides a window into a past sung by Strabp, Herodotus and Xenophon. It is a stirring on an ancient breeze when man first tamed the horse and dreamed of empires from its back. Perhaps it chants a lament for all lost species who disappeared because they did not evolve, or evolved too much and outstripped their environment.

The history of the Caspian is inseparable from the history of the Oriental horse because it is the quintessential Oriental horse.

Louise Firouz

Location map of Iran

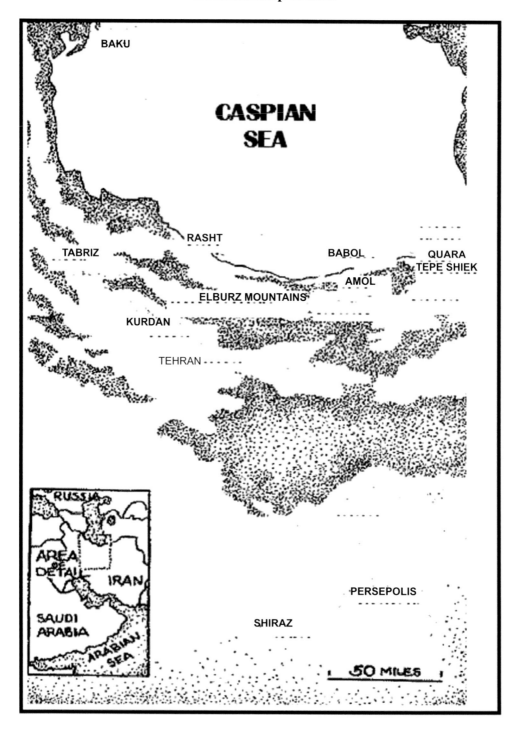

CHAPTER ONE

ORIGIN AND HISTORY

Rediscovery

Between the southern shores of the Caspian sea and Teheran lie the inhospitable Alborz mountains, amongst which the Caspian horse of Iran kept his identity hidden from the world at large for over a thousand years.

By tradition, Iranian children learned to ride on tall slim Turkoman mares and stallions, the alternative being a stocky 14 hand pony of Mongolian type, too wide for tiny legs to straddle comfortably.

Louise Firouz was a graduate at Cornell University, USA, studying Animal Husbandry, Classics and English. She married fellow student Narcy Firouz, an Iranian aristocrat, and returned with him to Iran where she formed a large Equestrian Centre.

She was determined to find something more suitable for her own two daughters and son to ride. Together with Joan Taplin, a Bermudan friend whose husband worked in Iran, Louise decided to investigate rumours that a small, narrow type of pony, known to local peasant farmers as 'Mouleki' or 'Pouseki' (little muzzle) existed in a small isolated pocket of the Mazanderan province. The area consisted of approximately 1,400 square kilometres of rice paddies, cotton fields and forests, beyond the Alborz range.

This sub-tropical, fertile, area of Iran affords excellent grazing in the spring and summer months. In the winter, snow and ice prevail and the Caspian has acquired a hardiness against the bitter cold of Iranian winters.

The journey, in April 1965, was unprecedented, uncustomary as it was for women to travel alone in Iran. As few feeder roads led from the coast road, they travelled by jeep until the mountain roads became inaccessible, when the party transferred to horses, using pack animals to carry their supplies. For several days they searched an area pin-pointed between the market towns of Amol and Babol without success. Just as they had resigned themselves to the probability that this was to be nothing more than an exciting adventure, rounding the corner of an Amol bazaar, a small bay stallion trotted serenely back into the twentieth century. Ostad*, though lice ridden and pulling an overburdened cart, was exquisite. He possessed an elegance and stature, which impressed Louise Firouz as befitting "something out of a Russian fairy tale."

Along with the stallion, Aseman*, and the mare, Alamara*, Ostad* was taken back to the Firouz farm, where they were found to be the perfect mounts for even the smallest child. Standing 11 hands high, Ostad* was narrow, fast, intelligent and spirited, but manageable and amenable, with incredible jumping ability.

Other expeditions followed but, despite extensive searches over the next two years, only very small numbers were found and rarely more than one in the same place. Those found were often covered in sores, lice, fleas and ticks, some sick and weak. They carried wood down from the mountains, pulled cotton planters or heavy carts, or were "plucked from the rice paddies" on the Caspian shore.

"We are still searching for Caspian ponies: diminutive... Arab-looking creatures with big bold eyes, prominent jaws and high-set tails, which so distinguish their larger cousins. It has been a losing battle as the already pitifully small numbers are further decimated each year by famine, disease and lack of care, until now we must accept the sad fact that the survivors must number no more than 30 ....."

(L. Firouz. PONY, December 1968)

The existence of this relatively unknown breed, in a land renowned for its love of magnificent horses, intrigued Louise Firouz. There was an elusive beauty and grace about this small horse, which did not seem to fit into the accepted picture of ponies. She was also puzzled by statements that the Arab horse was the oldest recorded breed in the world. They appeared to have been little known prior to the 7th century AD, whilst the Achamaenians, Assyrians, Parthians, Greeks and Sassanians were accomplished horsemen on somewhat magnificent mounts - judging from the reliefs and contemporary Greek writings which she had found during her research.

Early Research
Louise threw herself wholeheartedly into discovering the origins of the Caspian breed and whether, as she suspected, the little horse had preceded the Arab horse.
Prior to opening her Riding School, Louise and Narcy had lived for some years close to the ancient Palace of King Darius the Great at Persepolis. On the huge stone relief flanking the ancient staircase were carved a wealth of horse breeds including the Nisean horse, an impressive, powerful animal with a 'heavy' head. The Cappadocian, similar but lighter than the Nisean - the Chorasmian, Armenian, Scythian, Thracian - all recognisable breeds, were also represented. In sharp contrast the Lydian horse represented an unusual lightness for Archamaenian art and a smaller equine of Caspian size and type, with the prominent skull formation which proved to be present in all the artifacts resembling the Caspian found by Louise. There was no evidence of the Arab horse amongst the carvings at Persepolis, Shush or Ahki Bustam, which also depicted a small horse of Caspian type.

Links with Darius the Great
There could be no doubt that the little horse was highly prized. The trilingual seal of King Darius the Great, who had ruled Persia from 522 BC to 586 BC, depicted small horses of similar type drawing the King's chariot as he fired a barrage of arrows at a lion which towered over the tiny horses. (British Museum) That a King's fitness to rule was measured by his prowess at killing lions in his Persian game park, (the origin of the word 'paradise') reinforces the esteem in which he held the small horse. A larger or heavier horse could not have achieved the acceleration and manoeuvrability achieved by the athletic and courageous little equine
It was obvious too that King Shapur (AD 260) had also held the little horse in great esteem since bas reliefs at Naqsh-i-Rustam show a tiny horse carrying the King in triumph over the Roman Emperor Valerian, his feet almost touching the ground. The horse barely reaches the waists of his handlers. Another relief shows the Investiture of the first Sassanian king, Ardashir 1. The horses stand lower than waist high. (224 AD). Similar small horses appear at Bishapur.
Manmade objects such as a solid gold statue of small horses harnessed to a chariot (Oxus Treasure) are exhibited in the British Museum, and ancient writings, also evidenced the existence of a small equine of Caspian type dating from 3,000 BC to 500 BC. A terra-cotta

Foundation stallion Aseman* in Iran

Horses of Caspian type appear in the procession of tribute bearers carved on the staircase of the ruined Palace of King Darius the Great at Persepolis

plaque (2nd millenium BC Mesopotamia shows a small horse ridden with a nose ring (British Museum). It has the slim build and high tail carriage of the Caspian and is undoubtedly a horse rather than an onager. All recorded the exaggerated forehead formation, small ears and fine limbs.

Archaeologists, Zoologists, hippologists, specialists in chromosome, haemoglobin and bone, carried out research programmes, including Duerst, Coon, Clegg (Liverpool University).

Mrs. Mary Littauer, an internationally acknowledged American authority on the early history of the horse, offered to fund research into the osteological remains found at various locations. The excavation of a Median site at Hamadan led by David Stronach, Director of the British Institute of Persian Studies, revealed some 10,000 bones - amongst them were specimens thought to be those of the early Caspian horse. Bones found at Hamadan and Shahir-e-Kumnis (Parthian) were subsequently studied by the world renowned zoologist Sandor Bokonyi of Hungary. Having differentiated the bones of a very light small pony from those of the onager, Bokonyi was also able to identify bones belonging to two larger breeds of horse, one 14 hands and the other 15 to 16 hands. From this, he concluded that the three separate breeds were present at the same place, suggesting that the Persians were the first people to breed "consciously" at the beginning of the first millennium BC. Bones of the Arab horse were not present. This research also proved that the horses depicted on the friezes at Persepolis, 2,500 years ago, did exist and were not 'imaginary' and that the Persians valued the Caspian horses sufficiently to breed them deliberately along with the more 'useful' larger animals. It seems likely therefore that they were valued for their intelligence, agility and boldness, whilst hunting lions and for ceremonial purposes.

Similarities with the Arab horse

The bone structure of the Caspian is that of a horse - not a pony - in perfect proportions. The skull is unlike that of any other horse apart from the Arab.

Of the Arab horse, W.R. Brown wrote :

> "The first point of excellence looked for is that the forehead should exhibit a bulge between the eyes up to a point between the ears and down across the first third of the nasal bones - a formation of the frontal and parietal bones in the form of a shield known as the 'jibbah'."
>
> (1948 - The Horse of the Desert, New York)

> "This vaulted development of the forehead, so prized amongst lovers of the Arab horse, is present in the Caspian to a degree unknown in other breeds, even the Arab. Both possess characteristic dense fine bone, narrow hard hoofs and high set tail. Since these were not characteristics of the Indo-European import to the Middle East (2000 BC) it is proposed that the Caspian horse - a remainder of an ancient, isolated population in Iran was the wild stock from which the Arab was bred."
>
> Louise Firouz

Of the first 14 foals bred by Louise Firouz at Norouzabad between 1965 and 1970, only one did not exhibit "Caspian" characteristics, small ears, slim dense bone, oval-shaped hoof but - above all - the exaggerated bulging forehead which distinguished them from all other foals.

The ancient cylindrical Seal of King Darius the Great - 500 BC - shows a pair of tiny horses of
Caspian type harnessed to the Kings's chariot at a lion hunt
(Courtesy of the British Museum)

Small horses of Caspian type were portrayed in gold as part of the Oxus Treasure -
5th - 4th Century BC   (Courtesy of the British Museum)

Differences between the Caspian and other horse breeds (apart from those characteristics present in the Arab) :

1. There is a bulging of the parietal bones resulting in a pronounced elevation of the forehead and a marked difference in the length of the parietal bones forming the roof of the head, which continue to the back of the skull instead of stopping short of the poll. There is no parietal crest. (see Chapter 8)
2. An extra molar exists in the place where 'wolf' teeth might appear in other breeds. This is usually shed at two years with the milk teeth.
3. The shoulder blade is narrower at the top and wider at the base.
4. The cannon bones are longer and slimmer.
5. The first six vertebrae are longer than usual, giving the appearance of higher withers and a flatter back.
6. The hoof is narrow and oval and rarely needs shoeing. Front and hind hooves are similar in shape.
7. The frog is less pronounced in the Caspian than in other horse breeds.
8. The differences in haemoglobin are classed as "unique".

Manuscripts dated two centuries BC provided proof that horses of Caspian type had existed in the Kermanshah area of Iran at that time. Timotheus (6th Century AD) stated that a small breed of horse was present in the Kermanshah area: "The horses of the Medes are of moderate size with small ears and heads unlike those of a horse". This then does not place them in the area where they were found in 1965 by Louise Firouz. However, Noel (Geographical Journal 1921) writes:

> "The natives of the Kaler Dasht are a tribe that originally was brought over from Kermanshah, but it is so long ago now that they have lost their tribal characteristics and have settled on the land, mixing with the ingenous population. Besides their barley cultivation and their sheep and cattle they bred ponies".

There is no recorded trace of the Caspian from the time of the conflict between Islam and Mongolia (7th century AD) which resulted in the destruction of a great many libraries and museums, and the Caspian horse was largely ignored for over a thousand years. For Louise Firouz the obvious question was "how did these horses reproduce in the wild or semi-wild in which we found them " (since they rarely roamed together), "as there were normal sized horses with some 'Caspian' characteristics".

Louise concluded that "the Caspian was a strong genetic recessive, which occasionally bonded amongst two phenotypic mongol-type horses to reproduce a phenotypic Caspian which, when bred to another Caspian produced a genotypic Caspian". Despite the fact that some of the Caspians which Louise found had been running wild with larger horses, (and therefore may have been crossbred), all of the ones she bred to another Caspian produced true Caspian type.

The peasant farmers of the Caspian littoral stated that a normal sized mare and stallion would sometimes produce a miniature of Caspian type. Crucial to the survival of the breed

Relief at Naqsh-i-Rustam shows King Shapur (AD 260)

The distinctive domed forehead of a Caspian foal - Spark Shiraz
(dam - foundation mare, Shirine*)
Courtesy of the Ormskirk Advertiser

was the fact that eastern countries do not castrate their stallions as a matter of course, as we do in the west.

Louise Firouz was now satisfied that the Caspian was a true hot-blood. The research that she had implemented pointed to the possibility that it was an original of one of the four groups of horse/pony, his descendants including the Arab and thus the Thoroughbred, influencing in varying degrees many of our modern horse and pony breeds.

Independent theories

Theories resulting from research work carried out by Professors Speed, Skorkowski and Ebhardt of Edinburgh, into bone structure, resulted in the definition of four distinct types of wild horse (The Horse Through Fifty Centuries of Civilisation - Anthony Dent - Phaidon 1974.) These theories and those of Elwyn Hartley Edwards, a well known equine historian, matched almost exactly the results of research instigated in Iran.

Pony Type 1	Exmoor Type - not more than 13 hands
Pony Type 2	Taller and heavier - almost Mongolian in appearance
Horse Type 3	15 hands - large head and long back
Horse Type 4	12 hands - This type was described as 'Arab' before the rediscovery of the Caspian

'Horse' Type 4 was said to have the potential to increase in size, unlike Pony Type 1, which would just simply become fatter under better conditions.

Elwyn Hartley Edwards (Horses - Their Role in the History of Man - Willow Books 1987) relates this fourth HORSE type directly to the "Caspian horse of Iran".

"Horse Type 4 .... with an admixture of Type 3 of Central Asia, is the probable prototype (of the Arabian or oriental horse). Horse type 4 is certainly recognisable as Arabian and no great stretch of imagination is needed to perceive a possible relationship between the Arab horse and the rediscovered Caspian pony of Iran"

It is interesting that although only 12 hands, type 4 is described as 'horse type 4' and not 'pony'.

> "It had a high wither, slender legs, a straight or even concave profile, a high carriage of the tail, broad forehead, tapering skull with swelling muzzle and a level croup. We may call it the primeval Arab. As to the tendency to increase or decrease in size, we may put it this way, speaking of a series of generations as if they were the history of a single horse: an Exmoor taken off the heather into lush pastures is still an Exmoor, but a gross one; an Arab taken off the desert and acclimatized to County Meath grassland becomes more and more like an Anglo-Arab in structure and conformation."

This could account for the three quite distinct types of Caspian now developing in the UK - the finer, desert type, the slightly less delicate animal and the taller, stronger animal, which is more akin to the Thoroughbred horse or the Anglo Arab.

"Within the breed there is a natural gradation from a larger, stronger type to a dainty fairy-like type. This variety is a strength not a weakness".   E. Alderson - International Caspian Stud Book

Elwyn Hartley Edwards also places the Nisean horse and another, resembling Horse Type 4, in the Hamadan area of Iran where Bokonyi had identified a small horse and those of two other breeds, i.e. a horse of 14 hands or thereabouts and another of 15 - 16 hands.

"Assyrians recognised the need for larger horses which they produced by improved methods of horse management .... The breeding grounds of the Nisean horse were in North Western Iran around Hamadan in what was ancient Media. In the heat of summer it was possible to drive the horses up to the cool rich pastures of the foothills, where alfalfa or lucerne, a nutritious, high protein food, exceptionally well suited to the rearing of young stock, was grown.... This paragon amongst horses was a peculiar amalgam of blood. There was a relatively small indigenous horse in the region, having the characteristics of Ebhardt's Horse Type 4 and a decidedly Arabian look about it, and the steppe horse. Possibly the crossings, carried out selectively over a period of fifteen hundred years, included infusions of the Mongolian wild horse. This would certainly account for the stronger, even courser appearance of the Persian horses, which were of a type less refined than those depicted by the Assyrians but with their own particular elegance. Out of this jigsaw came ultimately the Turkmene and that golden horse, the Akhal-Teke, both renowned for their speed and stamina."

This would appear to suggest that not only did the Caspian horse play a part in the ancestry of the Turkoman and Akhal-Teke horses but also the heavier war horses used by the Persian armies.

Earlier sightings
Prior to the re-discovery of the Caspian, in the early 1950's, Elwyn Hartley Edwards had become interested in a breed of horse in western India, which were distinguished by the emphasized curve of their long ears. Whilst in India he became intrigued by one small horse which was totally unlike the rest of the pony or horse population. It had few of the conformation faults common to Indian horses and was a stallion, which was also unusual. It had short ears set on a quality head and a surprisingly free gait for so small an animal. He made enquiries as to the origin of the horse, which he now refers to as the 'Lucknow Caspian' and established that the horse had been bred outside India and had probably arrived with a caravan from the north west,

"a region adjacent to what we think was the breeding area of the Caspian. Whether he was, indeed, a Caspian horse, or something closely related to it, we shall never know ...   For centuries, certainly from the time of Alexander the Great, horses were brought into India through Kabul and via the Khyber as well as further south through Baluchistan. They were horses of distinct 'Oriental' type, Turkmenes, Uzbegs, Kabuli, Karabakhs and so on, most of which border on the Caspian Sea, the area in which Louise Firouz made her discovery".

In the latter part of the nineteenth century a small horse was identified in Western Iran by Wilkens. This he called Equus fossilis persicus (Persicus was the prefix used by Louise Firouz for the registration of her Caspian foals) and is almost certainly the early wild horse of Iran (Caspian). In 1904 a small horse of oriental type was discovered in Anau (southern Turkmenistan). Duerst labelled his find, Equus caballus pumpelli. It is possible too that small equines from ancient Persia reached many other countries via the Silk Roads. The Greek Pindos ponies are Oriental in type and the Greek 'Treasure of Vix' (fifth century BC) depicts ponies of Caspian type. Bactria (now Northern Afghanistan) was originally a province of Persia which once warred with the Greeks. Bactria was also the junction for several trade routes, the route to the West leading onto the Iranian Plateau. Whilst the Parthian horsemen were able to prevent Rome from gaining territory, they were aware of the advantages of allowing the Romans to conduct east-west trade across their territories. This trade included horses. Horses of Caspian type appear on several Roman artefacts, including ones depicted in museums at Hadrians Wall in Northumbria.

In 1998 a small pocket of horses of distinct Caspian type were discovered in China by John Schneider-Merck, who is funding the search for Caspian foundation stock in Iran. Research is being instigated to determine whether there is a genetic link between these horses and the Caspian horse of Iran.

'Tootoo' Iman, an authority on the 'blood' horse in India, and author of 'Newmarket and Ferghana', considers that the Caspian resembles the Turkoman rather than the Arab. He speaks of the Manipuri (small) horse, which is also reminiscent of the Caspian, with the same athletic skills; excelling at Polo.

Recent Research at Kentucky University

Compelling though the evidence was, further research would be needed before the horse world could be presented with the theory of a possible link between the Caspian and the Arabian horse.

In 1990, Dr. E. Gus Cothran of the Department of Veterinary Science at Kentucky University, Lexington, USA, began a research programme into the ancestral role of various horse breeds, including the Caspian horse, using DNA and genetic markers, in order to establish:

a) Conservation of genetic variation in rare breeds.
   (Reduced reproductive performance and increased disease susceptibility are associated with lowered genetic variation).
b) To determine genetic relationships among domestic horse breeds.
   As a possible ancestor to the oriental hot-blooded horses or a relict population, the Caspian is especially important in determining what ancestral horses may have been like.
c) As part of an overall genetic study of the domestic horse, the Caspian could reveal new variants to add to the current information available for horses.

In addition, the study of Caspian horses could indicate possible matings which would result in foals susceptible to neo-natal erythrocytoses. If blood groups were known, incompatible matings could be avoided.

Blood samples from 53 Caspians in England and 41 in Iran were flown to Kentucky for analysis. Samples were also frozen in the UK, for possible analysis at a later date, by Ken Jones of Edinburgh University, although to date it has been impossible to undertake this project as sponsorship has never been found.

Louise Firouz also supplied blood samples from Kurd, Persian Arab (unmixed with western blood), Turkoman horses (including Yamoud, Akhal-Teke, Goklan, Jargalan and Yabou). Following tests on these horses, and the Caspian, Dr. Cothran was able to state in a dendogram based on a phylogenetic reconstruction of the Oriental horse group, that the Caspian and Turkoman populations he had studied were in the most ancestral positions.

"Therefore we are able to state without doubt that:

1) A tiny form of horse existed in ancient Persia
   That this horse is the same as the modern Caspian and is ancestral to all forms of Oriental horse.
2) That the Turkoman existed in its present state at least as early as 3000 BC and that it also is ancestral to the Oriental horse."
   Louise Firouz

Research at Kentucky is ongoing. Its importance to this book is evident and the most recent results of the work of Dr. E. Gus Cothran, who has developed a very strong interest in the Caspian, are documented in the final Chapter

മോ

CHAPTER TWO
THE CASPIAN IN IRAN AND EXPORTS

Louise Firouz

Louise Firouz had become familiar with Iran at an early age. Her father was a lawyer from Washington, USA, who practised there for several years. After her marriage to Narcy Firouz the couple raised horses at Shiraz, close to the ruins of Persepolis. Seven years later they established a large riding and livery centre at Norouzabad, on the outskirts of Teheran.

Between 1965 and 1974 Louise found 27 Caspians and bred a further 32. Most of these she had purchased from peasant farmers, who found them more economical than their larger cousins, and who had used them for winnowing rice, hauling carts or as pack animals. Most were rescued from a life of overwork, disease and illness.

Louise carried out local research into the existence of the small horses, which she had never seen described in books and of which there was no more than isolated local knowledge. Apart from the feral stock, she discovered that, in Amol, the Caspian was sometimes bred to one of his own type due to the need for small cart horses which could dart in and out of the bazaar with more speed and accuracy than the more usual donkey. In Babol, the Caspian was occasionally crossed with a Mongolian or Tarpan type to increase the size.

Because of the poor winter forage, foals were usually left on their dams over winter so that they would have the benefit of their mothers' milk. It was probably because of this, and the lack of nutrition, that the mares usually only bred every other year.

The animals were broken at a very early age. From as young as eighteen months old some of the Caspians which Louise found had pulled heavy carts and toiled under over-laden pack saddles, carrying produce, tools and sometimes the farmer as well, for many miles between fields. It was common practise for the saddle and its load to be left on the animals following their return home. This meant that pressure sores never had the chance to heal. When too weak to continue working, the ponies would supplement the family table, out of necessity rather than indifference on the part of their equally overburdened owners.

Use of the Caspian at Norouzabad

Despite their earlier lack of care, the first five Caspians to arrive at Norouzabad quickly responded:

> "Rest and good feeding produced immediate results and gentle treatment overcame their initial suspicions and fears. They became affectionate and interested companions for children and delightful rides. They are built to carry the weight of a child with the gaits of a horse and, except at full gallop, at the speed of a horse, as I have established on our farm at Teheran. They could in fact become perfect children's ponies, if steps were taken to preserve the breed, which, I fear, is in serious danger of extinction."   Louise Firouz

Under the dry conditions at Norouzabad, the Caspians were fed a diet of blue grass and clover pasture, supplemented with alfalfa, which proved to be adequate to keep the active little horses in the peak of fitness in the riding school. Their feet were hard and strong and never required shoeing. Louise found that their strength and stamina belied their delicate looks and that they could easily carry an average adult. They took part in jumping competitions, competing (and often winning) against much larger horses. The Firouz family regularly went on rides together, mounted on Caspians. They were used extensively in the riding school, where even the stallions were ridden by children as young as five years old. Although spirited, they had a kind disposition and were easy to handle. The stallions were ridden in company with mares without trauma and were turned out together with no more than playful interchange.

It was little wonder that the Caspians had remained hidden for so long. "Having returned time and time again", on foot and on horseback, "squishing through the swamps of Mazanderan where the ponies winter", Louise and her family found a total of ten Caspians. Hoping for more success, they decided to forego "the spirit of the chase and the excitement of the showring for the search for ponies, following the herds of mares and foals into the summer grazing grounds." (Louise Firouz)

Four adults and seven children (five of them under nine years of age) travelled for the first six hours by Land Rover to a village in the mountains where 13 horses and donkeys awaited them. Unable to reach the camp site, they slept in a peasant hut:

> "anyone who thinks Persia is a land of heat and desert has but to sleep uncovered
> in the middle of the summer to discover the true extent of the delusion".
> (Louise Firouz)

Shooting their own food along the way, they waded through rivers and encountered steep ravines, down which they lost one of the pack horses. Amazingly, they managed to recover the animal to find that it had survived the 100 foot sheer drop, suffering only minor injuries. During the course of the journey they had guns, shoes and cameras stolen and were eventually deserted by their guides. Deep in thick forests, a location which Louise described as a naturalists paradise, they saw maral (red deer), wild boar and even a bear but only one of the 70 mares and foals they encountered on the trip even vaguely resembled a Caspian.

First Exports
In order to establish purity of the strain, Louise entered the horses she had found in a stud book, commencing in 1966, when she sold Jehan*, a beautiful liver chestnut stallion to Kathleen McCormick, a close friend of hers, in Great Falls, Virginia, USA.

In 1970 Joan Taplin, an American friend, whose husband had been working in Iran, returned to Bermuda, via Washington. Louise accompanied her on the trip, combining it with a visit 'home" and taking with her two in-foal mares, Mitra* and Momtaz-e-Mahal and a stallion, Daria Nour* (Dusty). In Washington, her daughters Roshan and Atossa competed successfully on the mares at local shows. Daria Nour*, a spectacular jumper, was barred on the grounds that he was a stallion.

When Louise and her daughters returned to Iran, the three Caspians accompanied Joan Taplin to Bermuda where she bred two colts, Amu Daria and Darius, and two fillies, Vashta and Roshan.

The gift of a mare and a stallion to H.R.H. Prince Philip
In 1971, the Shah of Iran celebrated the anniversary of the Peacock Throne, so called because the Naderi throne of 1798, which is embossed with over 25,000 precious stones, and the back of which includes sapphires and turquoises, is patterned in the shape of a peacock's tail.

The main events took place amongst the ruins of the ancient palace of Persepolis, from which Louise Firouz had first drawn inspiration as to the origins of her small horses. In it's heyday it survived four monarchs, eventually succumbing to fire (accidentally or otherwise) during the reign of Alexander the Great in 330BC. Its majestic pillars and vast stone carvings, however, had survived 2,500 years of Persian monarchy with dignity. Still, the tribute bearers, from the 28 lands which formed the empire, were clearly carved. They carried or led their gifts, including the small horses of Caspian type, to the great Persian King, along the stone walls leading up the double staircase, wide enough for horses and chariots to pass with ease.

It was a dazzling occasion. Hundreds of yellow and blue circular tents covered a vast acreage at Persepolis. Each tent had the capacity of a small bungalow. Representatives from almost seventy countries attended, together with their retinues.

H.R.H. Prince Philip and H.R.H. Princess Anne were amongst the many world dignitaries attending the celebrations. Prior to the start of the proceedings at Persepolis they spent two days in Teheran. The Princess was invited to participate in a ride across the plain of northern Iran towards the foothills of the Alborz mountains, accompanied, amongst others, by Narcy Firouz and his daughter Roshan, mounted on a Caspian horse. The Princess, who rode one of the Shah's finest stallions, expressed her surprise at the ability of the Caspians to keep up with the rest of the party.

> "In the group that went out that day, two riders were mounted on Caspian ponies. These small horses are famous for their size and toughness. They are pony size ... but they look like miniature horses with fine heads and legs. On this day one was ridden by a child of twelve and the other by an adult."

That she was impressed by their courage is also evident from her book "Riding Through my Life", in which she continues:

> "Below us was a near-vertical scree slope, becoming less steep as it reached the edge of the plain. I was a little disappointed that we would have to return the same way, but the ride had been worth it for the view. You might be able to imagine my surprise and trepidation when our guide walked his horse straight off the edge of the escarpment, followed by the other members of the party. This was obviously not the moment to demur as my horse seemed very keen to follow his friends. I assumed that he had done this sort of thing before, so I let the reins go loose and shut my eyes. Apart from keeping him straight, the rest was downhill.
> "We regained the floor of the valley without any mishap and made our way back to the stables at an extended canter, led by the Caspians."

When Prince Philip expressed an interest in the Caspians, he was invited to see a small number of them, which had been housed at the Royal Stables for the occasion and in order to take part in one of the many organized events; a race between the Norouzabad Caspian stallions. The jockeys were children of 5 years old. During the visit HRH voiced his concern at the small numbers in existence and particularly at the vulnerability of a breed whose entire reserves were all together in a single location. It was his involvement with the preservation of rare breeds that prompted Prince Philip to accept the present of a pair of Caspians - the lovely Arab-like chestnut foundation mare, Khorshid Kola* and the stallion Rostam, both

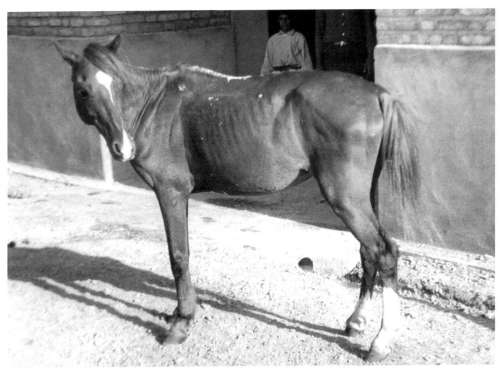

An early find - Shahryar (Holly) on arrival at Norouzabad

Shahryar - following rest and care at Norouzabad - ridden by Roshan Firouz

15

Ostad*, the first Caspian found by Louise Firouz in 1965 - ridden by Atossa Firouz -
"a small bay stallion out of a Russian fairytale"

Koh-i-Nour - ridden by Atossa Firouz at a gymkhana in Teheran

Foundation stallion, Daria Nour* exported to Bermuda and subsequently to the UK

Ruba*, foundation stallion at Narouzabad
His son, Ruba ll, was Supreme Pony Champion at
the Salon du Cheval in Paris (1974) and was later
exported to Australia

Zeeland*, foundation stallion - the only Caspian
retained by Louise Firouz during the ten year
ban on horse ownership - now owned by the
Ministry of Jehad

17

of which have had a marked influence on the breed today.

Accompanied by Louise, they travelled to Alag in Hungary, where they were quarantined, during which time the filly, Atesheh, was born. It was two years before the horses finally reached England. The quarantine laws were later changed so that subsequent shipments were quarantined at their destination stables.

Formation of the Royal Horse Society of Iran

In 1973 The Royal Horse Society was formed by the Crown Prince H.I.H. Prince Reza Pahlavi for the preservation of native species.

At that time Louise owned 23 Caspians including those she had bred. She had also sold five to private owners and three to the School of Veterinary Medicine at Pahlavi University. The Royal Horse Society purchased the 23 Caspians owned by Louise Firouz on the understanding that the horses would remain in her care.

In the summer of 1974, financial pressures forced her to sign an agreement selling the Norouzabad Equestrian Centre to the Royal Horse Society. The agreement allowed that she would continue to run the Centre and the Caspian Stud for a term of two years.

Despite the agreement, colossal feed bills mounted and remained unpaid by the Royal Horse Society, along with the salaries of grooms and instructors. Whilst Louise struggled to continue the breeding programme and accumulate further stock, The Royal Horse Society rapidly appeared to be losing interest in the Caspians.

During 1972, a stud had been formed in Great Britain with the stock from Bermuda and the loan of Prince Philip's Caspians. Now the stud contacted Louise, who was only too anxious for more bloodlines to be exported and, following tenuous negotiations with the Royal Horse Society in Iran, a small shipment of Caspians were exported to Great Britain in March 1974.

In October, the Royal Horse Society took possession of the Riding Centre for less than the price they had previously agreed. Louise and Narcy were given eleven days in which to vacate Norouzabad and to take with them the Caspians acquired, or bred, since the sale of the original herd to the Royal Horse Society, and the rest of the school horses. A penalty was payable for every day that the Firouz family, and upwards of 100 horses, cows, sheep, farm machinery and feed, remained at the farm. At the eleventh hour, a temporary refuge was found for the horses, in the mountains at Jaffarabad, whilst Narcy found rented accommodation for the family in Teheran.

Ironically, whilst the evacuation was taking place, officials of the Royal Horse Society were watching Ruba II, a Caspian stallion which they had purchased from Louise, winning the Supreme Pony Championship at the Salon du Cheval in Paris.

The evacuated Caspians spent the winter at Zarrindasht, a remote village in the mountains. Visiting the breeding stock became increasingly difficult, as snow piled higher on roads that were barely passable at best, and the journey from Teheran became almost impossible. Louise was filled with admiration at the stoicism of the peasant community and she learned to love the lifestyle which she and her family were eventually to adopt in order to keep their beloved Caspians. As the grip of winter forced the wolf population nearer and nearer to human habitation, Caspians and their keepers listened from the comparative safety of crude buildings as hungry wolves hurled themselves against heavy doors, barred against determined attack.

(left to right) Vashta, Mitra*, Momtaz-e-Mahal - shortly after their arrival from Bermuda

Touran - exported with the second shipment to the Caspian Stud UK in 1975 -
this line is threatened in the UK

19

In the spring she renewed her efforts to find remnant stock. She sought and obtained permission from the R.H.S. to register any new Caspians she could find.

From the summer of 1975 the refuge hosts were no longer able to look after the herd. In desperation, Louise moved the in-foal and nursing mares to the garden of the family home in Teheran, whilst the remaining Caspians were housed in a caravansarai in Southern Teheran - fly-ridden, traffic-congested and without grazing.

At this point Louise came very close to abandoning the entire venture and would have sold the Caspians there and then, had it not been for a visit to the races. Following the suggestion of a Turkoman friend they met there, Louise and Narcy purchased a 15 hectare farm at Ghara Tepe Sheikh on the Turkoman Steppes, next to Russian Turkmenistan. Whilst Narcy carried on his Construction Company in Teheran, visiting the farm at weekends, Louise looked after the horses and the land, making regular visits into Teheran. In wet weather the passes were treacherous. In winter, when they were impassable by vehicle, part of the journey had to be made on horseback. In Ghara Tepe Sheikh the new herd of Caspians grazed under natural semi-nomadic conditions, watched over by two Turkoman 'chaparders'. In summer, the family lived 'under the sky' on raised structures and in winter they inhabited a room at one end of the animal barn which protected them against the intense cold and the constant threat from wolves. Leopards too were not averse to picking off the odd dog.

By 1976 the new herd numbered twenty mares and three stallions. Three of the mares and a stallion were 'ear-marked' for the Caspian Stud UK They were moved seasonally. Summer was spent on the lush alf alfa pastures of the Alborz foothills and in the fall they grazed the harvested wheat stubble on the Turkoman Steppes. During winter days they grazed shoots of green barley planted especially for them. During the Spring of 1976 the herd grazed the lush pasture of the Khalet Nevi mountains, on the Russian border. Twice the herd was attacked by wolves. Two mares and a foal, which had been destined for the UK, were killed during the attacks, along with one of Louise's large riding horses. The remaining Caspians were returned to the safety of their winter quarters where it was impossible to maintain them indefinitely. At the same time Louise was concerned that the stock purchased by the Royal Horse Society were not being properly maintained and that it was becoming even more essential to preserve a nucleus of bloodlines outside Iran.

Further exports
In 1974, Louise had sold a stallion, Mehregan, to the USA and in 1975, the mare Nourie was sold to Venezuala. A further small shipment of Caspians was also exported to the UK, the majority of which were mated with UK stallions before being shipped to Australia. Amongst the number that she sold in Iran was a black stallion, named Prince Caspian. He was trained as one of Iran's famous dancing horses, usually performed by the elite of Arab stallions. This eventually led to his part in 'La Fille Mal Gardée' with the Sadlers Wells Ballet in 1977.

&⊃Q₰

CHAPTER THREE
TRANSFER OF RESPONSIBILITY FOR PRESERVATION

Export to the UK following wolf attacks

Louise requested that the Caspian Stud UK should take as many Caspians as possible as a matter of urgency. In place of the intended shipment of four Caspians, the stud agreed to purchase seven mares and a stallion.

Despite the haste, it was some time before negotiations with the Iranian Authorities were complete and the Caspians were only able to leave Iran in November 1976.

Crated together for travelling, the in-foal mares, stallion and yearling waited whilst a series of problems prevented them from being loaded onto the plane at Teheran airport. Take-off time was subject to a strict deadline, after which the plane would be grounded. Louise made several abortive attempts to load the ponies. Watching the whole affair with great interest from aboard the plane was Elizabeth Mansfield of the Rotherwood Stud in England, who was on her way home following an extensive lecture tour. She was actively discouraged from filming the episode by what she had mistakenly thought to be a pair of Iranian out-riders wearing pistols at each hip, who, catching sight of her camera, sped towards her, waving pistols in the air and threatening her with jail.

Delayed by several hours, the plane finally left Teheran airport with only minutes to spare. For obvious reasons the Caspians in this shipment were tagged 'the wolf batch'. Louise Firouz accompanied the flight and, having safely deposited the Caspians in their new home, departed for the London Hospital and a serious operation.

Nationalisation

Following a slow and uncertain recovery, Louise returned to Iran to face the wrath of the Royal Horse Society. Incensed by publicity generated by the arrival of the Caspians in England, they 'nationalised' all the remaining stock belonging to Louise, confined them at the prestigious royal stables in Gonbad-e-Ghabus, and forced Louise and her daughter to stay and look after them. After four months they were abruptly dismissed, following which the Caspians were almost totally ignored and suffered malnutrition and starvation.

Revolution and decimation of the herd

Between 1974 and 1978 Louise had found 27 foundation Caspians and bred a further 14.

During the latter half of 1978 the spark of revolution, which was to end the rule of the Shah, was already kindling. Louise and her daughter visited the stud and, finding the animals in a barbed wire enclosure without either food or water, registered complaints with all the revolutionary channels they could identify, without result.

After the departure of the Shah in January 1979 the remaining Caspians were auctioned off, without Louise being informed. The low asking price brought them within financial reach of a nomadic tribe, who purchased all but three of them, probably for meat. Two were turned loose to fend for themselves on terrain which was unlikely to support them. As far as Louise could ascertain at that time, only one stallion survived. The Shah's elite riding horses fared no better.

Ban on keeping horses

The new regime held the view that, despite the hard work to which these horses were subjected, they were the "playthings of the rich" and could not be afforded the valuable grain needed for the people. A subsequent ban on keeping more than one horse made it impossible for Louise to continue. Louise kept the grey Caspian stallion, Zeeland*. Zeeland* had been purchased by Helen Rattray, who had visited Louise in Iran and had also purchased a small number of Caspians from the UK Helen had, as his name implies, bought him with the intention of taking him back with her to New Zealand. The Iranian Authorities banned his export and, after keeping him for some time, Louise sold him to a neighbour who subsequently sold him back, finding that the little stallion had "too much energy". The ban on keeping horses remained for almost ten years.

Apart from those she had exported, the range of bloodlines, so painstakingly sought and preserved over fourteen years, were lost. Responsibility for the preservation of the breed now lay heavily on the shoulders of a small number of owners in the UK, Australia and New Zealand, particularly the Caspian Stud U.K, who also had charge of HRH Prince Philip's Caspians.

During the revolution, the bulk of Caspian records and photographs were destroyed and both Narcy and Louise were subjected to various terms of imprisonment. Being an American in Iran at that time singled Louise out, whilst Narcy's link with the aristocracy brought its own problems for the Firouz family. During one term of imprisonment Louise went on hunger strike and, being naturally tall and slim, was finally released resembling a 'bean pole'. Roger Cooper who was sentenced to 'death plus ten years' in Iran, was eventually released after five years but, during his term of imprisonment, the authorities found amongst his possessions a manuscript which Louise had loaned to him about the development of the Caspian. This was translated into Persian and several question sessions were devoted to the Firouz family.

Apart from Zeeland*, the stables at Ghara Tepe Sheik remained empty. Following the start of the Iran/Iraq war, petrol became strictly rationed and the seven hour journey between Ghara Tepe Sheikh and Teheran became impossible. Narcy and Louise bought three hectares of land, 45 kilometres west of Teheran in the village of Kurdan. Here they built a house and stables and, along with Zeeland, within the sound of falling enemy bombs, moved in to await the end of the war.

Re-establishment of a herd in Iran
The first Caspian born in Iran following a ban of almost ten years
During 1986, towards the end of the Iran/Iraq war, three mares, Kouchoulou* (chestnut), Balsaghar* (chestnut) Parissima* (grey) and a black stallion, Secandar Gol*, were found by nomadic horse dealers and taken to Kurdan.

On the 9th February 1987, a chestnut filly, Fereshteh (fairy) was born to Balsaghar* and Secandar Gol* at Kurdan. Louise discovered that the Iranian Horse Society had in its possession, Alvand (Ostad* x Pourandokht), one of the stallions which had been owned by the old Royal Horse Society and he also found his way to Kurdan.

During the war with Iraq, the revolutionary forces had made a wide sweep of the Caspian area, rounding up every wild or loose horse they could find. The animals had been used in the war effort as pack animals, transport, meat and, fortunately without much success, to trigger the detonation of land mines. The remainder of these animals, totalling almost a thousand, were housed in two huge corrals. At the cessation of hostilities Louise was invited to inspect the herd to see if any of the smaller horses contained could be Caspians. Amidst the dust stirred up by thousands of galloping hooves, 25 totally wild animals were lassoed from motor cycles by the revolutionary guard, tied and 'lifted' onto lorries. Fifteen of these were purchased by Louise and taken, along with the small number at Kurdan, to Ghara Tepe Sheikh.

Out of the fifteen she bought, Louise found that only six mares and a stallion were of true Caspian type. The rest were broken and sold as riding ponies.

In 1989, with eight mares and three stallions, Louise began her third attempt at breeding Caspians in Iran. However, the ban on exports remained and it seemed unlikely that any new bloodlines would be made available to the West.

It was shortly after this that illness struck again and Louise slipped quietly into hospital in the UK for a further serious operation and a shadow of the former Louise returned to Iran three months later.

1994 Shipment of new bloodlines to the UK

In 1993, Louise's daughter, Roshan, married to David Reddaway, the then British Ambassador to Iran , applied, at the end of a term of office, for permission to bring home a number of Caspians. These, she had helped to raise, partly at her parents' farm and partly in the idyllic 40 acre Embassy compound at Gulhak, a village to the north of Teheran, on the lower slopes of the Alborz mountains.

In July 1993, a truck, loaded with seven Caspians, alfalfa and water for the journey, left Kurdan for Brest, on the Polish/Russian border, en route to the UK. The journey took them via Baku, through wartorn Azerbaijan and Georgia, across the Caucasus mountains and through the Ukraine to Belarus. Louise was refused permission to travel with them on the grounds that she might be considered a desirable hostage by the warring factions. Despite having survived the journey through a country locked in conflict, they had not eluded the Caspian 'jinx'.

Following the relaxation of quarantine laws throughout the continent, the introduction of the EVA virus had shaken the British breeding industry. The Caspians were subjected to stringent tests both in Brest, where they were forced to remain for several months, and again following their arrival in the UK, on 22nd February 1994. Delay followed delay as rules were, once again, virtually written around the shipment.

Louise had travelled to the UK at Christmas, hoping to welcome the Caspians to their new home. Despite delaying her return flight she finally departed for Iran, before the arrival of the Caspians, on the 16th February, to find Narcy seriously ill. He died shortly after her return home and once again the herd was under threat. As part of the estate, it appeared that the horses would be sold to a wild life reserve, where they would have to take their chance against mountain lions but would at least have the chance to breed. However, even this advantage could prove short-lived because of the inevitability of in-breeding.

Meanwhile the horses that Roshan had exported to the UK had to be sold due to an immediate posting to Argentina. They met with little enthusiasm. The financial recession in the UK led to a depressed horse market and breeders feared the implications of imported stock following the EVA outbreak i.e. whether the Caspian Horse Society would allow the stallions to be used. As breeders knew so little about the virus there were fears as to whether horses tested clear could be carriers; whether foals could be affected etc. Finally, the sale of the stock incurred a heavy financial loss for the Firouz family.

Liz Alderson with HRH Prince Philip's mare, Khorshid Kola*
- foal Hopstone Zara by Ruba II
(Courtesy of Birmingham Post Studios)

Louise Firouz with foundation mare Balsaghar* and Fereshteh
- first foal born in Iran following the ten year ban on keeping horses

The present position in Iran

Sale to the Ministry of Jehad.

In 1995, the Ministry of Jehad expressed an interest in the Caspians and, at a fair price, purchased 37 Caspians and their foals, the majority of known Caspian stock left in Iran at that time. 11 of these were Foundation stock.

Foundation Bloodlines in Iran in 1994

STALLIONS	origin
Zeeland* (Grey) MJ	pre-revolution stock
Secandar Gol* (Black) MJ	Turkoman Steppes
Sohrab* (Bay) MJ	War release
Alvand (Ostad*xPourandokht)	former Iranian Royal Horse Society
Seezdah*MJ	

1995
Abdullah* *(Grey-circular white marks)   horse dealers

MARES

Kouchoulou* MJ	Babol horse dealers
Balsaghar* MJ	Babol horse dealers
Taraneh* MJ	War release
Khorshid* MJ	War release
Roxshaneh* MJ	War release
Khormalou* MJ	War release
Marium Khanum* MJ	War release

MJ - Sold to Ministry of Jehad 1995

Mr. John Schneider Merck, a friend of the Firouz family, with business connections in Iran, was keen to establish whether any remnant stock existed in the remote mountain regions. He approached Louise about the possibility of her maintaining a new breeding herd on his behalf. Again, a slow trickle of stock began to reach Louise via the horse dealers from which she had previously purchased foundation Caspians. Funded by John Schneider-Merck, whose father was a Veterinary Surgeon, involved in the evacuation of Lippizaner horses during the Second World War, the Caspians are examined thoroughly for type and defects before they are added to the growing herd being cared for by Louise and her grooms. Any deviations from type and quality are discarded, as are individuals which do not breed true to type. Some of the younger animals, in particular, arrive in very poor condition and not all survive.

The Ministry of Jehad have maintained the 'Persicus' herd and are keenly involved with the breed, working alongside Louise to establish an equine research centre in Iran. Hopefully, in the future, a number of second generation animals will be released for sale outside Iran, although, sadly, the trade ban between the USA and Iran excludes sale to American breeders.

෴

Persicus Yussef - exported to UK from Iran 1994
(Courtesy of Ann Priest)

Persicus Kuchek Khan - exported to UK from Iran 1994

Foundation stock in Iran - owned by John Schneider-Merck under
the care of Louise Firouz (1998)

(inset) not
all survive

Colt, Teo, with owner, Teo Schneider-Merck - Iran

30

CHAPTER FOUR
THE CASPIAN BREED IN THE UK

Foundation lines imported

Between 1971 and 1976 nine Caspian stallions and seventeen mares of Iranian origin were exported to the UK by Louise Firouz, representing 19 foundation bloodlines. A number of these had first been loaned to, or were bred in, Bermuda. Some of the mares carried in utero foals to Iranian stallions. One of the stallions (not foundation) was later gelded. Two of the stallions and three mares were re-exported to Australia. The majority of stock was purchased by The Caspian Stud UK . (see page 32)

In 1994 a further three mares and four stallions were exported from Iran.

Imports from Bermuda

Mrs. Joan Taplin, who had been a member of the search party which had first located the Caspian in Amol in 1965, returned to Bermuda in 1970, taking with her the in-foal mares Momtaz-e-Mahal and Mitra*, and the stallion Daria Nour*. In 1972 she sold the first two foals, Amu Daria (colt) and Roshan (filly), to Mrs. Mary Niebel of Pembury in Kent, England.

After reading a letter in 'The Field', which included a photograph of the two Caspian arrivals, Mrs. Elizabeth (Liz) Alderson (ex-Haden) then living at Shifnal in Shropshire, was completely won over and had soon decided that she was going to own and breed Caspians. Liz visited Mrs. Niebel, who subsequently offered to sell the pair to Liz and her mother, Mrs. Stephanie Jenvey ('Jaffa'). Following the purchase, Liz and Jaffa received a phone call from Louise Firouz asking whether they would be interested in importing further stock from Iran. With this in mind, they approached Arthur Griffin, a family friend and a former Director of Dudley Zoo.

Arthur Griffin and his wife ('Twink') played a major part in the preservation of the Caspian, placing extensive resources at the disposal of Liz and her mother. When "Griff" died in 1987 the walls of his study were lined with early photographs of Caspian imports.

The Caspian Stud UK - Prefix 'Hopstone'

The Caspian Stud UK was based at Hopstone Lea, Claverley in Shropshire, home of Charles and 'Jaffa' Jenvey. Following the purchase of Amu Daria and Roshan, Liz Alderson wrote to Prince Philip telling him of the stud's intention to exhibit them at the Royal Show. In the absence of Prince Philip, The Crown Equerry, Colonel Sir John Miller, visited the stand and offered them the use of photographs of Prince Philip's Caspians for display. Soon afterwards he offered them the loan of the stallion Rostam and the mares Khorshid Kola* and Atesheh, the produce of which were to become the property of the Caspian Stud UK

FOUNDATION STOCK OF IRANIAN ORIGIN IMPORTED BY THE U.K.
BETWEEN 1971 AND 1976

FOUNDATION
STALLIONS

FOUNDATION
MARES

DARIA NOUR(B)*
PALANG*

MITRA(B)*
KHORSHID KOLA*
SHIRINE*
DOUEEZ*
FATEMEH*
TALOCHE*
PARI*
SIYAH GOSH*

STOCK BRED FROM FOUNDATION STOCK AND IMPORTED BY THE U.K.

* represents foundation stock   **imported** stock appear in **bold** type
 (although present in several imported stock, foundation lines are only mentioned once)
Hopstone Banafsheh was carried in utero from Iran via Taliyeh and is the only representative of the stallion Felfel to survive.

STALLIONS IMPORTED	MARES IMPORTED	STALLION foundation represented (not imported)	MARE foundation represented (not imported)
	Momtaz-a-Mahal(B) Ostad*		Alamara*
	Taliyeh		Jehan Afrouz*
	Touran		Anahita* (via Pourandokt)
Mehran		Aseman*	Mehri*
Rostam		Ruba*	
	Vashta(B)		
	Roshan(B)		
	Atesheh(H)		
	Susiana		
	Gulpar		
	Aloucheh		
Maroun			
Karoun			
Amu Daria(B)			
Darius(Later gelded)(B)			
Ruba II			Nour Jehan*

OTHER FOUNDATION LINES
          Hopstone Banafsheh Felfel*

Atesheh (H) was born in Hungary via stock presented to HRH Prince Philip during a two year quarantine en route to the
U.K.   (B) Born in Bermuda

First shipment from Iran - 1974

Following extensive communications with Iran (usually at around 3 a.m.) and endless reels of 'red tape', the first shipment of Caspians purchased from Iran by the Caspian Stud UK. arrived at R.A.F. Lyneham in March 1974.

The Ministry of Agriculture had insisted on the Caspians being kept in quarantine for some weeks prior to their departure from Iran and, in order to isolate them, Louise had taken them out to her farm on the Turkoman Steppes, making compulsory vetting procedures extremely difficult. She arrived at Teheran Airport on the appointed travelling date to be told that they would be flying from a different airport some miles away. On arrival she was re-directed to Teheran where, after loading the Caspians onto the aircraft, she was informed that it was too late for the flight to leave and the horses would have to remain crated on board until take off the following morning.

This first shipment from Iran to the UK included the dark bay mare, Taliyeh, who was to become extremely influential in the breed as the dam of seven stallions. Taliyeh, who was bred by Louise Firouz from her first stallion, Ostad*, and the mare Jehan Afrouz, bred a total of 15 foals. Her chestnut yearling son, Karoun, by Rostam accompanied his in-foal mother and her colt foal, Maroun, by Ruba 11. The other member of the shipment was the gentle iron grey stallion Mehran by Aseman*.

The Iranian Royal Horse Society also sent along their second groom, Mahamad, to teach the stud how to care for the horses. Unfortunately, Mahamad did not speak any English, so communication between them was limited to the content of Jaffa's small pocket phrase book.

Second shipment from Iran - 1975 and subsequent exports to Australia

In 1975 the Caspian Stud UK took delivery of four mares from Iran, Susiana, Gulpar, Aloucheh and Touran. These were covered by UK stallions and quarantined at Hopstone Lea, Claverley, before continuing their journey to Australia, with the exception of the delicate little grey filly, Touran, who was retained by the Caspian Stud UK . They had also arranged the purchase of Ruba II for Australia and kept him for six months, during which time he covered the UK mares, Taliyeh and Khorshid Kola*.

Importation of Bermudan foundation stock - 1975

Meanwhile, on Bermuda, a fuel crisis meant fewer flights, which in turn led to a feed crisis for livestock. With little grazing on the island, Joan Taplin was forced to part with the three, then rather lean looking, Caspians and their foals, Vashta (filly) and Darius (colt).

The Caspian Stud UK purchased the remaining stock, with the exception of Momtaz-e-Mahal, who was given to HRH Prince Philip by Louise Firouz. A luxury flight to England, in the passenger compartment of a scheduled Boeing Jumbo Jet, ran true to form. The plane developed engine trouble and had to make a forced landing at Kingston, Jamaica. Dusty (Daria Nour*) was a small, lively, black and brown speckled, grey stallion. He had a refined head and delicate in-pricked ears but above all he had an enormous jump. His son, Darius was a "bright glossy red bay". Mitra*, dam of Amu Daria, already purchased by the Caspian Stud UK, stood only a little over 10 hands and despite being 12 years old when she arrived in the UK, was a bundle of energy. She was a dark bay, with a lovely head and large eyes. Momtaz-e-Mahal was around 12 hands high, light bay, with excellent conformation and a rather shy temperament. Bred from Ostad* and

Taliyeh - in Iran - exported to the UK in 1974,
Taliyeh was extremely influential as the dam of seven stallions

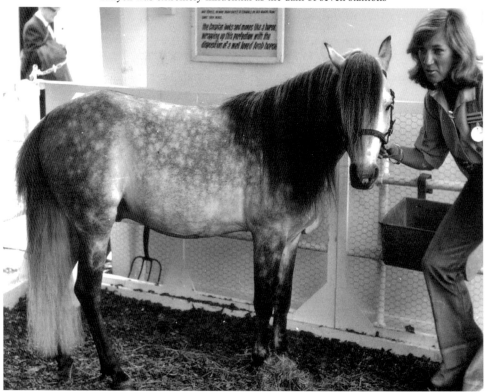

Liz Alderson exhibiting the imported stallion, Mehran, (Aseman* x Mehri*) at the
Royal Agricultrual Show, Stoneleigh, Warwickshire (Courtesy of the Farmers Guardian)

Alamara* in Iran, she was also loaned to the stud by Prince Philip, where she was ridden by Liz Alderson's young daughters. Vashta, the daughter of Momtaz-e-Mahal, a light strawberry roan, made up the shipment.

Emergency Shipment from Iran - 1976
(The 'Wolf' Shipment)

It was during a visit to London, to present portraits of Khorshid Kola* and Rostam, by Roy Reynolds, to HRH Prince Philip, that news of the wolf attacks in Iran reached Liz and Jaffa. The paintings were later displayed in the Royal Mews and at Windsor.

Following the conversation with Prince Philip and Colonel Sir John Miller, which concentrated mainly on the use of the Caspian for driving and, in particular, Rostam and Maroun (which were eventually driven as a pair by Ernest Long, Head Coachman at the Royal Mews) Liz and Jaffa telephoned Louise. Liz later reflected:

".... perhaps still affected by the Buckingham Palace euphoria, we decided to import a young stallion and seven mares on a flight tentatively booked in November."

This was to be the first phone call of many, which, despite the fact that she had become almost immune to shocks as far as importations were concerned, even Liz found disconcerting.

Awakened in their hotel room, close to Gatwick Airport, awaiting the arrival of the shipment, they were informed by the British Bloodstock Agency that the flight had been ordered to leave Iran without the Caspians and was then airborne en route to England. For four hours the hotel telephone lines burned with news that the plane was, and then was not, in the air! The Caspians were, then were not, on board!

The Caledonian plane finally arrived to be greeted by a 'morass' of television and press crews, the pilot having resolutely refused to take off without the Caspians.

"As is so often the way, the news of this dramatic decision achieved far more attention than our carefully worded portrait story. Newspapers all over the place, in particular the Sunday Telegraph and Observer, sobbed to their readers of dying breeds, savage wolf attacks, mercy missions, etc.

to such an extent that the television companies became interested and we became, for a short time, a most over-exposed piece of public property. "

Liz described the flight as :

"hurried, complicated and extremely expensive - again funded by courtesy of Griff (Arthur Griffin). The bay stallion, Palang,* and seven mares and fillies, several in-foal, arrived at Gatwick all in one crate, to a considerable press reception. With them was Louise, having lived through a nightmare of Iranian bureaucracy, intransigence and opportunism. As with all three importations there had been considerable delay, but the Caspians, as always, had weathered it without harm. Louise herself was quite ill, and left Gatwick for the London Clinic and a serious

Maroun - imported with his dam, Taliyeh, in 1974.
A ride and drive stallion and popular sire

Foundation stallion, Palang* - imported 1976 as part of the 'wolf' shipment- Palang* was longer
in the head than average but his overall conformation was good

Siyah Gosh* foundation mare imported 1967 - photo
Chris Shortis (from a painting by Josiphine Lely)

Rostam - presented to HRH Prince Philip
- Ride and drive stallion

Foundation mare Pari* owned by Lis Leich - the youngest of the original foundation stock,
Pari* was still breeding in 1998

operation. Again, this sort of brinkmanship and toughness is as typical of Louise as her beloved Caspians."

The stud decided to keep the Caspians together, loaded into one crate, for the journey home, rather than put them through the added trauma of re-loading. They were accompanied by the Ministry Vet (whose job it was to ensure that quarantine rules were strictly adhered to). It was 1.30 a.m. the following morning before a very *"expensive crate of horseflesh"* was unloaded. Before her departure, Louise revealed that the Caspians had only been allowed to leave on payment of a rather large sum of money.

The existing stud animals had been evacuated in order that the new shipment could be quarantined at Claverley. A four acre field, five minutes along the road, was loaned to them by Peter and Helen Southan. The stallions were mainly housed at Arleston Manor, Telford, home of Arthur Griffin and his wife.

It had already been decided that part of the new shipment should be sold, in order to recuperate some of the additional cost of the importation, along with the unique red and white hand-woven rugs and nose-bags worn by the Caspians during their flight.

This shipment included the stallion, Palang* and the mares Shirine*, Abrisham, Fatemeh*, Doueez*, Pari*, Siyah Gosh* and Taloche*. As there was a slight doubt as to whether Abrisham was 'pure' Caspian, and to avoid any possibility of introducing non-Caspian type into the breed, she was sold as a riding pony.

Louise's intention had been to breed from the original foundation stock and to send their progeny to the UK. At the time, the evacuation of foundation stock was a particular sacrifice for Louise and her herd in Iran. In the event, the shipment was fortuitous, since the foundation stock remaining in Iran were lost, making first and second generation stock already in the UK as important as the foundation shipment.

So far, the only foundation mare to come to the UK had been Khorshid Kola*, apart from the stock which came via Bermuda, (the mare, Mitra*, and stallion, Daria Nour*).

There was a marked difference between the 1976 foundation stock imported to the UK and stock which had been bred under the care and expertise of Louise Firouz. 'Jaffa' described the 'wolf' shipment as *"shell-shocked"*. Three of the foundation animals in particular, bore the scars of their early years.

Doueez*, a tiny mare, with the shyest of natures, had had the tips of her ears removed, probably as a means of identification. Her foals proved to have the most inpricked ears of all the Caspians.

The stallion, Palang*, was extremely headshy and was only bridled with great difficulty, crouching to the ground when touched. His head was not so refined as the other Caspians and he was not as easy to handle as most of the other stallions. He was also slightly larger and threw foals of the larger type. For these reasons some breeders felt unsure whether Palang could be considered a true 'Caspian'. However, his conformation was good and of typical Caspian type. The Caspian Stud UK, who had discarded Abrisham, fearing that she was not quite 'correct', and who also reluctantly gelded a foal carried in utero by the foundation mare Shirine* because of the height that it reached, were reasonably sure that Palang* was a true Caspian. Because he was so headshy, Palang* spent most of his life at the home of Arthur Griffin. He never fully overcame his fear and was never loaned out to other breeders. Amongst others, he produced two very successful stallion sons; Hopstone Shabdiz (out of

Stallion, Runnymede Orion (left) - the mare, Spark Shimari (centre) and two of her
foals by Orion were part of the first shipment to Norway in 1998
(photo: Brenda Dalton)

The Author with foundation mare, Shirine* rescued from life as a pack animal in Iran and
exported in 1976 as part of the 'wolf' shipment   (Courtesy of the Ormskirk Advertiser)

Khorshid Kola*) and Hopstone Jamshyd (out of Hopstone Zara - Ruba II x Khorshid Kola*). Both stallions are the larger type and both have been breed Champion. Hopstone Shabdiz is extremely important to the breed in the UK as he is the only son of Khorshid Kola* in the U.K, her only other son having been sold to New Zealand. Shabdiz was purchased as a yearling by Eric Worthington (Working Hunter Pony judge) and his wife, Mavis, who broke him to saddle and harness. He was subsequently sold to the Henden Stud.

Shirine*, a delicate little mare of unique colouring (light red dun), had been found with an open wound on her spine, having carried a heavy pack saddle from the age of eighteen months. As a result, her joints and spine were affected and she moved with a 'running' action. She also suffered severely from stress colic. The foals she produced were usually larger than herself and the foal she had carried in utero from Iran grew to be several inches taller than herself. Determined to keep the breed true to type and fearing (despite Louise's protests) that she may have been covered accidentally by something other than a Caspian, Liz had the colt gelded. The next foal that she produced (by the larger stallion, Palang*) was also larger than Shirine* and by the time the stud realized their mistake, Sheikhan, in all probability sired by Aseman* in Iran, had already been gelded. Aseman* was lost in the revolution, leaving only his son, Mehran (first UK shipment), to represent his line, although Fatemeh* and Doueez* both produced 'in-utero' fillies to Aseman*.

Post Revolution Responsibility

The Caspian Stud UK became the prime owner of Caspians outside Iran and, during the years immediately following the Revolution, were mainly responsible for the preservation of the Caspian. They bred, or were responsible for the breeding of, 56 pure bred Caspians before the death of Jaffa's husband, Charles Jenvey, in 1981, and subsequent death of Arthur Griffin, in 1987, forced the stud to run down and finally give up breeding following the death of the mare Taliyeh in 1990. Along with the other founder studs, they bred most of the stock which now forms the basis of the pure bred Caspian Register. The Caspian Stud UK were responsible for displaying Caspians on the Royal Showground, Stoneleigh, for eighteen years, starting from the year in which they took delivery of their first two Caspians.

Without the intervention of the Caspian Stud UK it is doubtful whether the breed would be in existence today.

Promotion of the Breed

Alongside the responsibility of breeding, The Caspian Stud UK ran an impressive promotion and performance campaign. (Chapter 9) During these first years Liz and Jaffa inspired a great deal of interest in the breed. They arranged for Caspians to appear on a number of T.V. and radio programmes, endless publicity articles and the use of Caspians by top 'names' in the world of driving, jumping and showing. Liz formed the British Caspian Trust (later The British Caspian Society), the Caspian Stud Book and, with the assistance of Louise Firouz and Lawrence Alderson (then Technical Consultant for the Rare Breeds Survival Trust) for the first two International Caspian Stud Books. (Liz became Mrs. Lawrence Alderson in 1984.) She was also responsible for the early Newsletters and all registrations until 1982.

Constant media interest surrounded the early Caspians, which were photographed frequently and included in new editions of breed books, Hamlyn's 'Wonderful World of Horses' (stallions Mehran and Maroun and yearlings Atesh and Mustapha), 'The Young Rider's Handbook' (foundation mare Shirine*) and many others. Horse & Hound wrote a major article on the breed on February 3rd 1980, followed by Hoofprint (March/April), The Ark, (March/May) and Pony World (May). The Warwickshire Agricultural College made fact-finding visits to the stud and Liz and Lawrence visited the Central Veterinary Laboratories in Weybridge and the Equine Research Station. Newmarket, who both offered advice regarding genetics.

Elwyn Hartley Edwards, an equine historian and author of many books, who has included the Caspian in several of his historical works, took a keen interest in the Caspian and judged at the Caspian Breed Show at Stoneleigh in 1987.

Lawrence Alderson, an international authority on genetics, assisted and advised the British Caspian Society towards becoming a charitable trust and suggested a genetic breeding policy for the breed.

The Animal Health Trust at Newmarket hold records of bloodtyping which were commenced on behalf of the Royal Horse Society of Iran. As well as Caspians, these include Turkoman and Arab specimens, taken in 1978 - a project cut short by the subsequent Revolution.

The Caspian took part in numerous Rare Breed Parades, including The Muschamp Stud, Fulmer and Windsor. Breed classes were held at the British Show Pony Society Area Show, Shrewsbury, and at the Ponies of Britain Annual Summer Show, Peterborough. Although Caspians were still in very small numbers, the shows were well supported, mainly by the Caspian Stud UK, Lis Leich, Vikki Shortis, Muriel and Rosemary Harris and the Henden Stud.

The Crown Equerry, Colonel Sir John Miller, has always been, and still is, a stalwart supporter of the Breed and the Breed Society. He has worked tirelessly on behalf of the Caspian and, at his own request, is still kept up to date with the ongoing work and policies of the Caspian Horse Society.

In the summer of 1981 Louise Firouz was allowed to leave Iran in order to attend her daughter's wedding. Her husband, Narcy, was kept under house arrest during her absence. After visiting her family in the USA, Louise and her daughters, Atossa and Roshan, returned to the UK in time to watch the Caspian classes at Peterborough. During the visit Louise Firouz and Liz Alderson wrote the Caspian Breed Standard.

Following the death of Charles Jenvey in November 1981, 'Jaffa' Jenvey decided to move out of 'Hopstone Lea' and into a cottage in the grounds. This resulted in a loss of grazing, which forced the stud to scale down their breeding programme. Some of the mares, including Taliyeh, were leased to breeders, on a two year term basis. The Caspian Stud UK covered the mare with a stallion of their choice. After foaling, the mare was covered again by the lessee and, at weaning, the first foal was returned to the Caspian Stud UK.

In 1985 the stud lost the use of their rented grazing land near the village of Claverley. Taliyeh returned to Hopstone but most of the other mares and stallions were loaned out to suitable breeders. In most cases this worked extremely well and some of the mares were subsequently purchased by their lessors.

Following the death of Arthur Griffin, in 1987, the grounds of his home Arleston Manor, Telford, Shropshire, were no longer available for the grazing of youngstock and for the stallion, Palang*. Arthur Griffin lived just long enough to learn of the birth of the first foal in Iran following the ten year ban. Following his death Jaffa Jenvey wrote :

"... it is safe to say that without 'Griff's' intervention and support there probably would be no Caspian horses in England. His financial and active support in the first four importations from Iran and Bermuda ensured there were sufficient breeding lines available here, and undoubtedly saved the Caspian horse. It was Griff's great enthusiasm and dedication which enabled Liz and me to go out to Australia and New Zealand to check on their Caspians which had been bred at our stud. He was so proud of the rescue, and so happy to do anything possible to help the Society. For years his company, Dart Spring, sponsored the Caspian stand at the Royal Show at Stoneleigh. It was Griff who organised our successful raffles and 'blackmailed' his friends to give lovely prizes."

"The walls of his house are covered with photographs, recording the very start of the 'Caspian Rescue'. With Griff's untimely death, the Society has suffered a very great loss...."

Palang* joined the Iranian mare, Taliyeh, at Claverley. Maroun and Touran were both out on loan. Touran and Palang* died in 1989. Taliyeh did not long outlive them. She died, having foaled every year except one, in 1990. The stallion, Maroun, remained on permanent loan to Mrs. Pamela Thomas, a former Chairman of the Caspian Horse Society Council, until his death in November 1995. Maroun threw consistently good stock and sired twenty six foals, all of which are noted for their small size, temperament, conformation and action.

Of the early years, Liz reflects :

"Mum and I had a great deal to learn about horse breeding, despite having kept horses for many years. It is to their immense credit that the Caspians put up with our often bungling attempts to propogate their species with such patience and good humour. The stallions were especially forgiving. We also learnt - first from Louise and then from our own experience - that, except in the breeding season, Caspian stallions liked to run together for company. Many of the older stallions liked nothing better than a colt to teach. Mehran and Maroun were especially good in this respect. The stallions were also far happier when working at other things besides stud duties and most were broken to Ride and Drive. We found that their high intelligence and kind natures made them very quick to learn and easy to handle".

1994 Imports from Iran

A new shipment of Iranian bloodlines, three mares and four stallions, arrived in the UK early in 1994, at a time when, despite Government re-assurances, the British public remained unconvinced that the country was lifting out of economic recession. Caspian breeders were not finding it easy to sell stock advertised for sale within the UK and were cautious about putting mares in foal.

In addition, a virus, thought to have been imported from Europe, had affected a well known Sports Horse Stud Farm in the Midlands. The EVA virus was an unknown quantity in the UK and its implications were part of an on-going discovery process. There were no Rules in place for the testing of imports. Individual Horse and Pony Breed Societies had to draw up and apply new rules of their own in order to safeguard breeding stock. The movement of horses and ponies had been curtailed, often voluntarily; horse shows and other equestrian events had been cancelled in affected areas, in order to try to contain the virus. Caspian buyers were extremely cautious about purchasing stock from outside the UK and the result was a financial disaster for the Firouz family.

Following extensive tests, the stallions Persicus Kouchek Khan and Persicus Yussef were purchased by a sponsor in the south of England and leased to Naomi Thomas, who now owns them, whilst the rest were advertised for sale by tender. Henden Stud purchased the stallion, Persicus Nicky and two mares, Persicus Ai Banou and Persicus Khoshgel Khanum. Louise's daughter, Atossa, retained a mare and stallion, Persicus Tehou and Persicus Amir, which she took with her to Belgium, Tehou having first been covered by one of the Henden stallions.

STOCK BRED FROM FOUNDATION STOCK IN IRAN AND EXPORTED TO THE U.K. IN 1994

STALLIONS IMPORTED	MARES IMPORTED	STALLION FOUNDATION LINES REPRESENTED (not imported)	MARE FOUNDATION LINES REPRESENTED (not imported)
	Persicus Ai Banou		
	Persicus Khoshgel Khanum	Zeeland*	Marium Khanum*
	Persicus Tehou		
Persicus Kuchek Khan		Secandar Gol*	Balsaghar*
Persicus Amir			Taraneh*
Persicus Yussef		Sohrab*	
Persicus Nicky			Khorshid*

* represents foundation stock
bold represents imports

foundation lines are listed once only
Persicus Tehou and Persicus Amir are owned by Atossa Firouz in Brussels.

Exports to the USA
During 1994 and 1995, 32 Caspians were exported to the USA. from the UK. In addition, 18 were purchased from Australia and New Zealand. During subsequent years, sales to the USA have accounted for a major proportion of UK youngstock and by the beginning of 1999 there were upwards of 200 Caspians in the USA.

CHAPTER FIVE
UK Studs

Runnymede (Stud No. 3)
Muriel and Rosemary Harris

Following those of H.R.H. Prince Philip and the Caspian Stud UK, Runnymede Stud was established by Muriel Harris in 1974. Muriel purchased the stallion Karoun, which accompanied the first Iranian shipment, and subsequently purchased Hopstone Banafsheh, Taliyeh's (in utero) filly. Banafsheh, a striking dark bay, thoroughbred in appearance, is extremely important to the breed, being the only representative of the grey foundation stallion, Felfel*, to survive the revolution. She also purchased the filly Hopstone Shuka, out of Atesheh, the only foal sired by Darius (bred in Bermuda).

After three months in quarantine at Claverley, Karoun was moved to the Harris's home at Virginia Water. After two years at stud he was professionally trained for driving, when he proved to be completely safe on the roads and often driven in Windsor Park. There followed a further two years at stud where he sired foals, mainly to Section B mares, from which he produced remarkably Caspian type stock. Interestingly, he showed a distinct preference for Caspian mares. Muriel's sister, Rosemary, also became intrigued by the breed, adding her own expertise and preferences.

As well as being used for breeding, Karoun was broken to harness and Banafsheh to saddle.

Part-bred stock:

Muriel and Rosemary Harris have done a great deal to promote the part-bred Caspian in the UK, using Welsh mares with top bloodlines. By crossing and re-crossing the offspring with pure-bred Caspians, Runnymede produced stock which reached the standard required for Grading-up status, which was instituted as a precautionary measure in the early days in case a level of in-breeding should be reached which necessitated the introduction of new blood. The breeding policies followed by the early Studs ensured that this necessity never arose and some of these cross-bred ponies have been extremely successful both as performance and show animals.

Muriel and Rosemary Harris both served on the Council of the British Caspian Trust and on subsequent Councils. Rosemary was Secretary to the Caspian Horse Society for several years.

Up to 1998, twenty seven pure-breds had been bred by Muriel and Rosemary Harris, mostly traceable to Karoun or Banafsheh, using mainly Forstals Barewa as an outcross.

During the latter part of his life, Karoun stood at the Henden Stud, where he died in 1992. Karoun sired twenty three pure-bred foals, several of which became important stallions, including the New Zealand stallion, Hopstone Atesh (out of Khorshid Kola*) and the Henden Stud's home-bred stallion, Quasimi.

Runnymede Karamat, a chestnut stallion typically bred by Rosemary Harris, (Karoun x Runnymede Penny Royal (Forstals Barewa x Hopstone Banafsheh)) was amongst the first flights to the USA in 1994 as well as the fillies, Runnymede Camelia and Runnymede Beryl, bred from typical Runnymede mares.

Kineton
Suzanne Dore
Suzanne Dore purchased the foundation mare Fatemeh*. She also part-owned the imported grey stallion, Mehran, with the Caspian Stud UK, and used him extensively for driving as well as breeding, before his sale to the Henden Stud. Fatemeh was in foal to Aseman (the sire of Mehran) when imported. She produced five foals before her death, including Kineton Khamyab, a bay mare, exported to the United States in the 1970's, unfortunately producing no purebred offspring. Suzanne also leased Darius (bred in Bermuda), who had inherited his sire, Daria Nour's, spectacular jumping ability.

During the last few years of her life, Prince Philip's mare, Atesheh, was leased to the Kineton Stud where she bred several foals, including the stallion Kineton Khalif, who was included in the first shipment to the USA.

Suzanne has been closely involved with the Caspian since the breed was first imported into the UK She was a member of the original British Caspian Trust and has served on all subsequent Councils up to the present day.

Craythornes
Lonbay
The Lonbay family purchased several Hopstone-bred Caspians in the early days including Hopstone Parandeh (Mehran x Hopstone Zara), Hopstone Kandeh and Hopstone Asal. They also purchased the foundation mare, Taloche*, who bred only three foals before her death in 1982. Mrs. Lonbay bred eleven Caspians and played a crucial role in the early days of the Caspian in the UK

As their stud stallion, they kept the home bred Craythornes Xerxes (Hopstone Tavus x Taloche*), whose importance was obvious to the breed due to the rarity of the Taloche* bloodline. Sadly Xerxes died, having sired only two foals.

Costessa
Vicky Shortis
The Costessa Stud was originally an Arabian Stud located in Norwich, Norfolk.

The Caspian foundation mare, Siyah Gosh*, was purchased by Vicky Shortis when the New Zealand authorities refused to allow the importation of the mare into New Zealand. Siyah Gosh* has produced consistently good stock, mainly of the larger type. From Siyah Gosh* and her offspring, Vicky bred nineteen Caspians up to 1998 and has also served on the Caspian Horse Society Council for many years as Treasurer and Membership Secretary.

A Costessa bred filly was included in the first shipment to the USA

Winstay
Helen Keeling
Helen Keeling purchased the foundation mare Doueez* who died in the early 1980's having produced five foals.

Forstals
Lis Leich
The youngest of the foundation stock imported was the chestnut filly, Pari*, who was purchased from the Caspian Stud UK by Mrs. Lisbet Leich in Norfolk. She also purchased the mare Hopstone Sasha. Although Lis did not breed a large number of stock, she bred the stallion, Forstals Barewa (Daria Nour* x Pari*) who became one of the breed's most popular stallions, having sired more than fifty foals prior to his death in 1998. Barewa was part owned by Henden Stud, where he was kept at stud. Lis was one of the longest serving

members of the Caspian Horse Society Council upon her death in 1997.

Eastern

Jennifer Quinney

The Eastern Stud was established with stock purchased mainly from the Caspian Stud UK, including Hopstone Zara.

The stud stallion, Hopstone Jamshyd, is out of Zara, by the foundation stallion, Palang* and has been successfully shown in harness and in the show ring. Jennifer Quinney, a former show hunter rider, also owns the stallion, Middleton Shir.

The stud concentrates on turnout and performance and most Eastern stock are broken to ride and/or drive.

The importance of Henden Stud as a successor to the Caspian Stud UK

Jane and Ron Scott

The Henden Stud was originally based at Ide Hill in Kent and became the largest and most important Caspian Stud in existence.

Henden is owned by Jane and Ron Scott and, just as the Caspian Stud UK took over responsibility from Iran, for maintaining as wide a gene pool as possible, so the Henden Stud took over responsibility from The Caspian Stud UK.

Their breeding policy from the outset has been to exist as an independent body, working on the assumption that if there were no other Caspians available anywhere in the world, Henden could exist and expand on its own gene pool, without having to inbreed, unless for a specific purpose.

Ron and Jane (who trained in agriculture in Lancashire) were introduced to Caspians by the Caspian Stud UK on the Breed Society stand at the Royal Show, Stoneleigh.

In 1979 they purchased nine Caspians. Amongst these was the stallion Hopstone Shoja (Maroun x Siyah Gosh*), one of the smaller, lighter type of Caspian, who was, until 1995, the stud's senior stallion, with an exceptional temperament. Shoja still stands at Henden to a limited number of mares. In 1980, they added another seven to the stud and, in 1981, purchased the imported Bermudan mare, Vashta, from Alan Loades, along with a further two mares. The purchase of Hopstone Shabdiz (Palang* x Khorshid Kola*), two years later, gave them a base which included almost every bloodline available.

The stud keeps upwards of ten stallions at any one time. During the early 1990's they kept as many as 30 colts at livery, at a nominal fee, on behalf of other breeders, in order to avoid the necessity of gelding colts before maturity and before they could be properly assessed as stallions.

Henden Stud moved from Henden Manor in 1990 to Midway Manor, Bradford-upon-Avon, and is now based close to Chippenham in Wiltshire. At any one time, the stud numbers up to 100 pure bred Caspians, including stallions kept at stud on behalf of other owners and mares at livery or visiting.

There are very few of the older Caspian mares which Henden Stud have not had through their gates at some time. They have also stood most of the foundation or originally imported stallions at stud, including Rostam.

Whilst concentrating mainly on breeding, they regularly exhibit stock at various shows and exhibitions. During the years that the Society exhibited at the Royal Show, Henden stock was often evident on the display stand and Jane and Ron are usually 'resident' each year at the Royal Bath and West. Their stallion, Hopstone Tavus, won the stallion class at the Yelverton Show on every occasion that he was exhibited there. Hopstone Shabdiz was included as the 'fourth horse type' in the Celebration of the Horse at the Ascot Festival in 1998.

Hopstone Shoja, a perfect example of the smaller type Caspian, was exhibited at Essen Equitana, Germany in March 1985. Although a great deal of interest was shown in the Caspian stand, it was felt that unless Caspians broken to ride and drive were exhibited there for immediate sale, there was probably little hope of using the Equitana as a sales promotion exercise. It was for this reason that they returned to Essen in 1987 with gelding Hopstone Tarik, who was exhibited in harness.

Henden Stallions

Hopstone Shoja is the type of Caspian, which the stud would like to concentrate on breeding, as a matter of personal preference. Small (11.1 hands), light in limb and body, but with sufficient width to allow free movement, Shoja's temperament is outstanding, which Ron and Jane consider to be a priority. They are particularly pleased with Henden Quasimi, a stallion which they bred in 1989, sired by Muriel Harris's stallion, Karoun, out of the home bred mare Henden Soraya. Quasimi is a perfect example of cyclic crossing, as Soraya is by Shoja and is out of Henden Zimbabe (a Mehran x Hopstone Zardalu mare). Zardalu, now deceased, was out of Prince Philip's mare, Khorshid Kola*. Not only is Quasimi the type of Caspian, conformationally, which the stud aims to breed but he also displays the temperament of his grandsire, Hopstone Shoja. Quasimi, who stands 11 hands, has been handled with ease by Jane and Ron's daughter, Fleur, from the age of eight. Shoja's sire, Maroun, was also noted for his incredible temperament and tendency to throw smaller stock.

Although the stud prefer this type of Caspian, they stress the necessity to maintain a very full genetic base and try not to let their personal preference outweigh this balance.

The 12.2 Ride and Drive stallion, Hopstone Shabdiz, is sired by Palang*, noted for his size and tendency to throw larger stock. He also has an impeccable temperament and was Supreme Champion at the 1996 Caspian Breed Show.

Forstals Barewa (deceased 1998), stood 11.2 hands and was sired by the popular foundation stallion, Daria Nour*, who is also well represented in Australia through his son, Amu Daria.

The stud's Henden Zebedee, a very attractive 11.2 chestnut stallion by the home bred Henden Alpha - out of Hopstone Zardalu, was exported to the USA in 1998. Henden Stephen, an 11.2 grey son of Mehran, and his son, Henden Wenceslas, also stand at Henden, along with the dark bay Henden Noah (Hopstone Shoja x Henden Nicola) and the 1994 imported stallion from Iran, Persicus Nicky. A USA-owned son of Hopstone Banafsheh will also stand at Henden from 1999.

Henden have always been willing to make the stud available for research into the Caspian, and for pioneering work which might benefit the equestrian world as a whole. When one of their filly foals was found with a leg hanging helplessly beside her in the field, experience told them that the only course open to them was to have her put down. At the request of their vet, they agreed to take the foal, in the back of their estate car, to the Royal 'Dick' Veterinary College in London. Here the bone was plated and pinned (a technique used on the badly damaged leg of former motor cycle racing ace Barry Sheen). The foal was in plaster for 10 weeks before the success, or otherwise, of the venture could be measured. Henden Rebecca (Hopstone Tavus x Henden Roshana) made a complete recovery apart from a slight limp.

She has since bred several foals, which have produced offspring of their own, and continues to breed at Henden, owned by Fleur Scott, who, in 1995, started her own stud under the Lanhill prefix.

In 1990 Henden made available their entire herd of Caspians for bloodtyping when Mary Jo Kent, an expert in the field of DNA fingerprinting, took blood samples from 53 Caspians on behalf of Gus Cothran at Kentucky University. Most of the breeders whose stock were resident at Henden agreed to their Caspians taking part in the venture. At that time 70 Caspians were resident, including visiting stock. It was a marathon task, taking a whole day of non-stop stock-manoeuvring to complete. The samples were then rushed, via Rosemary Harris, to Heathrow Airport for the flight to Kentucky, where they were met by a representative from the University. The results are documented in the final chapter of this book. Testing now continues with stock exported to the USA.

Ron and Jane Scott have both served on respective Councils over the years, Jane, as Registrar, and Ron as Chairman of the Caspian Horse Society.

Starting with seven Caspians in 1994/1995, a considerable percentage of Henden bred stock has been exported to the USA. The stud also act as a collecting point for stock en route to the USA.

Other early Caspian breeders

Other breeders who played a short but crucial role in the early preservation of the Caspian are Elizabeth Gauvain, who bred Every Lara, a mare exported to New Zealand and Janet Ashton, who for a short time bred Caspians using the prefix Alpine. Jim Willetts owned the stallion, Amu Daria, before his exportation to Australia. Alan Loades bred Middleton Shir, a stallion broken for scurry driving, from the imported mare, Vashta, and Mrs. P. Hughes bred Chestnuts Soraya, out of Taloche*. Don Short owned the stallion Hopstone Mustapha and Hopstone Balsagher (now gelded). Helen Kemp, Helen Forsyth, Ken Evans and James Froggatt were also early owners who played a part in the preservation of the Caspian. The author purchased the foundation mare, Shirine*.

First foals upon which the breed is based

The foals produced over the first few stud seasons provided the breeding base for the Caspian horse, using (in the main) a system of cyclic crossing (described more fully in Chapter 8).

In November 1974, Khorshid Kola* produced a filly, Hopstone Zardalu, to Rostam, untimely, due to the fact that the mare and stallion ran loose together at Hampton Court over the winter, prior to their being loaned to the Caspian Stud UK. Zardalu, a lovely chestnut Arab-like facsimile of Khorshid Kola*, appeared with her dam on 'Midlands Today' at four days old. Sold as a foal to Mr. Ken Evans in Gloucestershire, she later became one of the most successful of the UK stud mares and senior brood mare at the Henden Stud. She produced ten quality foals, including the stallion, Zebedee.

On 3rd March 1975, Taliyeh produced Hopstone Banafsheh, the all-important filly foal by the Iranian foundation stallion Felfel*.

On the 20th April, Roshan produced a chocolate dun colt (Hopstone Zagros) to Mehran and on the 21st April, Atesheh gave birth to Hopstone Tochal, a colt foal by Amu Daria. Tochal was purchased by Jean Beer in Western Australia and became part of the first shipment, including the three Iranian mares, plus the stallion Ruba II, to be exported to Australia.

That the bloodlines of mares and stallions were of equal importance is demonstrated by the fact that the matings for that year were all to different stallions, with the exception of Rostam, who covered two mares.

1976 Foals

Dam	Sire	Name	Purchaser
Taliyeh	Amu Daria	Hopstone Mustapha grey colt	D. Short
Khorshid Kola*	Karoun	Hopstone Atesh ches colt	(NZ)
Roshan	Daria Nour*	no foal	
Atesheh	Darius	Hopstone Shuka cream filly	M. Harris
Mitra*	Mehran	Hopstone Sasha roan filly	L. Leich
Momtaz-e-Mahal	Rostam	no foal	
Vashta	Rostam	no foal	

1977 foals

Karoun and Mitra*, produced a tiny chestnut colt, Hopstone Kuchek. Atesheh produced a chestnut filly, Hopstone Firouzeh ('turquoise'), to Mehran. The two mares which the stud considered to be their best were covered by Ruba II, (winner of the Supreme Pony Championship at the third Salon du Cheval in Paris the year before), before his departure for Australia. Consequently, the resulting foals were of considerable importance; a bay filly (Hopstone Zara) was born to Khorshid Kola*. Hopstone Tavus, a bay colt, was produced by Taliyeh; a full brother to the stallion, Maroun, who had accompanied his dam to the UK. Zara produced Hopstone Parandeh in 1981 to Mehran. She was also the dam of the stallion Hopstone Jamshyd in 1983 and the filly Hopstone Phoebe in 1984. Jennifer Quinney purchased Zara, Jamshyd and Phoebe in 1985. Sadly Zara died after breeding only two foals for the Eastern Stud. Hopstone Tavus was purchased by Henden Caspian Stud. The imported mare, Touran, produced Hopstone Balsagher, a grey colt sired by Maroun.

The foals carried in utero from the 'wolf batch' were born in 1977. Fatemeh*, a four year old bay mare, bred a filly (Kineton Kistam, meaning 'who am I') by Aseman. Fatemeh was purchased by Suzanne Dore who, together with her brother and sister, John and Judith Fay, founded the Kineton Stud in Warwickshire. Shirine* (sweet), produced a colt (Hopstone Sheikhan) by Aseman. Doueez* produced the filly Roya (also by Aseman). Doueez* was purchased by Helen Keeling from Sutton Coldfield. Siyah Gosh* ('black ears'), who did not foal in 1977, was under negotiation for purchase by Helen Rattray in New Zealand . However, just as her stallion in Iran (Zeeland*) never reached her, neither did Siyah Gosh*, whose export was again blocked by red tape - this time from the authorities in New Zealand - and Siyah Gosh* remained in the UK, where, in 1978 she foaled a bay filly, Hopstone Talafi, to Palang*. Luckily, 1978 saw a high ratio of fillies to colts and several new owners and breeders. In 1979 Siyah Gosh* was purchased by Mrs. V. Shortis of the Costessa Arabian Stud. 7 fillies and 4 colts were born in the UK in 1980.

Along with a few more recent additions, these births have been the base upon which the breed, outside Iran, has been founded.

1978 Foals

Mare	Stallion	Foal	Owner	Comments/Purchasers
Siyah Gosh*	Palang*	Hopstone Talafi (bay filly)	Caspian Stud UK	
Taloche*	Rostam	Hopstone Rafiq (Bay colt)	Caspian Stud UK	Henden Caspian Stud (1980)
Khorshid Kola*	Mehran	Hopstone Safiyeh (bay filly)	HRH Prince Philip	Exp. 1978 NZ Mrs. H. Rattray
Atesheh	Maroun	Hopstone Siyakh (Ches. filly)	HRH Prince Philip	Mrs. J. Fountain-Barber
Mitra*	Palang*	Hopstone Seh-Shambe (bay filly)	Caspian Stud U.K.	Exp. 1978 N.Z. Mrs. H. Rattray
Taliyeh	Mehran	Hopstone Kaftar (grey colt)	Caspian Stud U.K.	Exp. 1978 W.A. Mrs. B. Gyles
Shirine*	Palang*	Hopstone Tanbaku	Caspian Stud U.K.	Sired one foal/gelded. sold H. Forsyth/P. Rene
Touran	Maroun	Hopstone Qahve (grey filly)	Caspian Stud U.K.	Exp. 1978 NZ Mrs. H. Rattray
Doueez*	Mehran	Winstay Khoshal (grey filly)	Helen Keeling	Henden Caspian Stud (1981)
Hopstone Zardalu	Hopstone Zagros	Alpine Zamira (ches. filly)	Janet Ashton	Zardalu was the first foal born in the UK (Khorshid Kola*)
Fatemeh*	Mehran	Kineton Kodam (bay filly)	Suzanne Dore Janet/John Fay	Only Fatemeh* progeny still breeding (1998)
Vashta	Maroun	Middleton Shir (bay colt)	Anthony Loades	One of only two foals produced by Vashta/ stallion, Eastern Stud

1979 Foals

Mare	Stallion	Foal	Owner	Comments/Purchasers
Khorshid Kola*	Karoun	Hopstone Shah-Zade (ch. colt)	Caspian Stud U.K.	died as foal
Taloche*	Daria Nour*	Hopstone Lili (bay filly)	Caspian Stud U.K.	Fran Smith-Boyes (now in France).
Touran	Palang*	Hopstone Chahar-Shambe gr. colt	Caspian Stud U.K.	Sired one foal. Gelded. Driven in tandem by owner Chris Belton
Taliyeh	Daria Nour*	Hopstone Capella gr.filly	Caspian Stud U.K.	Henden Stud (1979)
Siyah Gosh*	Maroun	Hopstone Shoja Bay colt	Caspian Stud U.K.	Henden Caspian Stud (1979) Senior stallion
Shirine*	Maroun	Hopstone Asal ch. filly	Caspian Stud U.K.	Mrs. D. Lonbay (1979) Alan Whitley (1994)
Hopstone Zardalu	Mehran	Kineton Ismalla gr. filly	Suzanne Dore	John/Janet Fay Sold to Henden then Eastern Stud
Momtaz-e-Mahal	Rostam	Every Vanya Bay colt	E. Gauvain	Henden Caspian Stud (1980)
Roshan	Maroun	Every Roshana Bay filly	E. Gauvain	Henden Caspian Stud (1980)
Fatemeh*	Maroun	Kineton Khamyab Bay filly	Suzanne Dore John/Janet Fay	Exp 1981 Mrs. L. Vaughan Canada
Doueez*	Maroun	Winstay Mehreban Bay filly	Helen Keeling	
Hopstone Banafsheh	Karoun	Runnymede Lalah Bay filly	Muriel Harris	
Hopstone Shuka	Karoun	Runnymede Tela ch. filly	Muriel Harris	
Pari*	Daria Nour*	Forstals Barewa Bay colt	Lisbeth Leich	Stallion - very influential

CHAPTER SIX
SOCIETIES AND STUDS SET UP ABROAD

CASPIAN PRESERVATION SOCIETY OF WESTERN AUSTRALIA
and MAJOR STUDS IN WESTERN AUSTRALIA

In 1975 Margot Schabort persuaded the Shah of Iran to sell Ruba II to her, in order to bring him into the disease-free environment of Australia. Although she paid an extremely high price for him, coupled with crippling travelling expenses, she never managed to use him. Whilst he was in quarantine with the Caspian Stud UK in England, Chris Lowe asked if he could keep him at stud in Victoria, where he spent five years, siring only part-breds.

He later sired the pure breds Marida Hushyar (Aloucheh) and Marida Yashaman (Susiana) from the imported mares at the Marida Stud (South Australia) and the pure bred filly Ruba's Gift (by artificial insemination) immediately before his death in 1993.

Margot also reserved Hopstone Tochal (a near black colt) and his sire, Amu Daria, along with three in-foal mares, but circumstances prevented her from purchasing Amu Daria and the mares, which were then sold to Ida Graham (Marida Stud) in South Australia.

Subsequently, Tochal was purchased by Jean Beer who leased him to Betty Gyles of the Heroden Stud.

STOCK EXPORTED TO WESTERN AUSTRALIA BY U.K. IN 1975
Bloodlines exported by U.K.

STALLION	MARE	FOUNDATION STALLION REPRESENTED	FOUNDATION MARE REPRESENTED
AMU DARIA		Daria Nour*	Mitra*
RUBA II		Ruba*	Nour Jehan*
	SUSIANA		Anahita*
	GULPAR		
	ALOUCHEH	Ostad*	Mehri*

Further stock, bred mainly by the Caspian Stud U.K., were exported to Australia, in 1978 although several of these Caspians were subsequently purchased by a stud in New Zealand.

HOPSTONE KAFTAR	Aseman*	Jehan Afrouz*
HOPSTONE TOCHAL		Khorshid Kola*
HOPSTONE ATESH(N.Z)		
	EVERY LARA(N.Z)	Alamara*
	HOPSTONE QAHVE(N.Z)	
	HOPSTONE SAFIYEH(N.Z)	
	HOPSTONE SEH SHAMBE(N.Z) Palang*	

Heroden Stud, Jarradale, WA - established 1976
Betty and Tony Gyles

Heroden Stud stood Hopstone Tochal to local non-Caspian mares until they imported Hopstone Kaftar in 1978. Tochal was then sold to Ray and Sue Eiffler at Narambeem.

They bought the mare Marida Pranses from Ida Graham's Marida Stud in 1981. Pranses bred only one foal (to Hopstone Kaftar) before a series of false pregnancies forced Betty to abandon breeding from her and to use her as a riding pony. Heroden Stud therefore bred only one pure Caspian, the mare Heroden Jinistan. Hopstone Kaftar was also bred to pure Caspian mares at Tandara Stud and sired one foal at the more recently formed Easterly Winds Stud.

Betty Gyles was responsible for extensive promotion work in Western Australia. She also established the Caspian Preservation Society of Western Australia in 1981.

The first two Heroden part-bred Caspians collected 44 rosettes at their first four shows, as three year olds. Only three weeks after he was backed, the stallion Hopstone Kaftar gave a riding display on behalf of a charity for the rescue of distressed horses. He went though a short programme of basic 'dressage' movements, then remained completely calm whilst his rider 'flapped' around in the saddle, slipped down his neck and lay backwards towards his tail, all at the trot. The demonstration was so well received that Betty and Tony Gyles were inundated with stud requests and turned the display into an art form. The stallions, Hopstone Kaftar and Hopstone Tochal, became part of a celebrated Caspian demonstration team which included a display of trick riding, vaulting, somersaulting backwards, swinging under the stomach, vaulting over the tail, tent pegging and riding in halters. Hopstone Kaftar was also driven extensively by Betty Gyles.

Tandara Stud, Narrikup, WA
Established 1981
Sue and Roy Eiffler
In 1981 Tandara bought Tochal from Jean Beer. They also purchased the fillies, Marida Khazar and Montaha from the Marida Stud. Marida Khazar suffered a fatal snake bite and was replaced by Marida Roya. In 1982 Tandara purchased Amu Daria from Ida Graham. These were followed by the fillies, Cheleken Musha and Cheleken Avvol Dokhter, and the stallion Cheleken Kabba (Hopstone Atesh x Hopstone Seh Shambe) from Helen Rattray's Cheleken Stud in New Zealand. Ruba II was also leased by Tandara for a short time. Hopstone Tochal was eventually purchased by Helen Rattray in New Zealand.

At the end of 1994, Tandara had bred a total of 24 pure bred Caspians and in 1995 seven Tandara-bred mares were exported to ProtoArabians in the USA.

Telopea Stud, Galston, WA
Established 1990
Telopia Stud was established in 1990 with the stallion Tandara Daric. They also licensed the home bred stallion Telopia Tousan by Hopstone Kaftar out of the New Zealand mare Cheleken Avvol Dokhter, which they also purchased from Tandara. Tandara closed in 1996 when Tousan, Daric and Cheleken Avvol Dokhter were purchased by the Markazi Stud in New South Wales.

Easterly Winds Stud, Herne Hill, WA
Established 1991
Joanna Mulcahy
Joanna purchased the only pure bred Heroden mare, Heroden Jinistan, and the Tandara mare, Bejestan. She also purchased the stallion Tandara Etan but Etan proved to be such a good riding pony that after using him for stud only twice Joanna made the decision to geld him so that he would be eligible to compete at Pony Club. Joanna Mulcahy had the loan of Ruba II at the time of his death and bred Ruba's Gift, out of Heroden Jinistan. Heroden Jinistan and Ruba's Gift were later sold to the Tandara Stud. Joanna exported the 1993 filly,

Summer Breeze, to the USA in 1995

Corinthia Stud, Southern Cross, WA
Established 1995
Belinda McNamara
The mare Easterly Winds and the colt Marida Safir were the founders of the Corinthia Stud.

SOUTH AUSTRALIA
(Australasian Caspian Society)
 The Australasian Caspian Society (Inc) was founded in 1980 by Mrs. Ida Graham,

> "to preserve the Caspian as a breed, adhering to the rules as stated by the Iranian and British Societies".

Marida Stud, Balhannah, near Adelaide, SA — Established 1976
Marshall Steer and Ida Graham (deceased) Mandy Miller
Ida and Bill Graham and partner, Marshall Steer (who bred Trotters and Appaloosas) and his wife, purchased the stallion Amu Daria from the UK in 1976. Almost immediately he was followed by the mares, Susiana, in foal to Maroun, Gulpar, in foal to Karoun, and Aloucheh, in foal to Mehran (imported from Iran via the UK), which Ida referred to as 'brides' for her beloved Amu Daria. Susiana was in foal to Maroun and foaled Marida Eskander (stallion). Gulpar was in foal to Karoun and foaled Marida Shereen (mare). Aloucheh foaled to Mehran (Marida Khass - mare).

After six years at stud, Amu Daria was the sire of all the stock Marida had bred. Ida therefore had to import another stallion and keep one of her young colts for use as an outcross. Amu Daria was sold to Tandara Stud in Western Australia in 1982.

In 1983, with the help of her husband and her partner, Marshall Steer, she imported Cheleken Avval Pesar from New Zealand to share stud duties with Marida

Balsaghar, a Champion first generation stallion bred by Ida and Marshall. She also bred two fillies from Ruba II.

Ida was responsible for the only embryo transfer involving Caspian horses, in 1988, when a fertile egg from the mare Marida Shereen and the stallion Marida Hushang was implanted into a two year old Clydesdale mare. The resulting pure bred filly (Marida Tarikh) proved to be slightly larger than a normally bred Caspian at birth but regained normal height during the first two years, during which she was placed first in the filly class at the Royal Adelaide Show.

Out of the 49 Caspians registered in South Australia, between 1978 and the end of 1993, 34 were bred by Marida, the last one bred by Ida being Marida Gilas, born in 1993.

Ida was over 80 and still very actively involved with Caspian breeding when she died in 1992.

A lovable and dynamic lady, Ida proved to be a mother figure and the major force in keeping the Society together. The Australasian Caspian Society maintain that "without Mrs. Graham's tireless efforts, Australia would have no Caspians." Mandy Miller, who played a major part in the embryo transfer project, took over Ida's interest in the Marida Stud.

Two Marida bred mares and a colt were sold to MCC Farms, USA, in 1995. Gulpar died in 1996.

54

Gruntal Stud (Green Valley)
Established 1981
Kurt Wehner
Between 1982 and 1988 Kurt Wehner bred six Caspians from the mares Marida Khass, Marida Talafi and Susiana (leased from Marida Stud). Talafi was sold to the Markazi Stud.
Stoneyfell Stud
Established 1982
J. Wilkinson
Stoneyfell Stud leased Marida Shereen in 1982. They also own the imported mare Aloucheh.
Chippendale Stud, Forreston, SA
Established 1981
A. A. Mann
Chippendale purchased Marida Malak (Amu Daria x Gulpar), the first Caspian to be born in Australia (1978). The stud are actively involved in showing, including the Royal Adelaide Show. Between 1984 and 1999 they bred ten Caspians.
Three Chippendale bred mares, a stallion and a colt were sold to MCC Farms USA in 1995. Four were by the Cheleken stallion Avval Pesar, and the colt, Chippendale Bahram (front cover) was by Marida Hushang.
Astara Stud, Forreston, SA
Shauna and Gerard Swart
Shauna and Gerard Swart were the Stud managers for Chippendale stud before founding the 104 acre Astara Stud. They leased four fillies from Stoneyfell Stud and purchased the mare Gruntal Frilia, a grand-daughter of Marida Khass (deceased) who was by the UK imported stallion Mehran, in order to try to preserve the Aseman* line in South Australia.
General
The vast distances involved have posed great problems in terms of breeding and competition work for owners and breeders in Australia.
The sales to the USA were timely, since they reached a stage when all their stock was sired by Cheleken Avval Pesar (Hopstone Atesh (Karoun x Khorshid Kola) x Every Lara (Rostam x Momtaz-e-Mahal)) Amu Daria (Daria Nour* x Mitra*) or Marida Hushang (Amu Daria x Susiana). The imported mares, Susiana (Rostam x Anahita) and Aloucheh (Ostad* x Mehri*) are still breeding.
Having investigated the feasibility of using A.I. from imported semen and discarded the possibility, South Australia desperately needed a new stallion. This situation is in the process of being rectified by the generosity of a US breeder.
Caspians were invited to take part in the opening parade of the 6th World Three Day Event Championships at Gawler. Six Caspians and their riders paraded as Snow White and the Seven Dwarfs led by a member dressed in Iranian Costume which was loaned to them by Roshan Firouz.
The most recent stud to be set up in Australia is Maureen and Bob Byrne's Markazi Caspian Stud, situated in northern New South Wales on the eastern coast, the most highly populated region of Australia. The stud is named after the Markazi province of Iran, meaning "central". They have combined bloodlines from Western and Southern Australia and are responsible for a Caspian slot on the Internet.

Western Australia - Hopstone Kaftar (Mehran x Taliyeh) - ride and drive stallion
Exported from the UK and owned by Tony and Betty Gyles

South Australia - stallion Marida Hushang by the exported stallion, Amu Daria (Daria Nour* x Mitra*) out of the exported Iranian mare, Susiana (Rostam x Anahita)

NEW ZEALAND
STOCK EXPORTED TO NEW ZEALAND from the U.K.

STALLIONS	MARES	MALE FOUNDATION LINE REPRESENTED (not imported)	FEMALE FOUNDATION LINE REPRESENTED (not imported)	
HOPSTONE ATESH			Khorshid Kola*	
		Ostad*	Jehan Afrouz*	
			Ruba*	Mitra*
	EVERY LARA		Alamara*	
	HOPSTONE QAHVE	Aseman* Mehri*		
			Anahita*	
	HOPSTONE SAFIYEH			
	HOPSTONE SEH SHAMBE	Palang*		

CHELEKEN
Helen Rattray

In 1977 Helen Rattray imported the UK stallion, Hopstone Atesh. In 1978 she visited Louise Firouz in Iran and purchased the grey stallion Zeeland. The publicity surrounding the 'wolf' importation was still fresh in the memories of the Iranian authorities and he was impounded by the regime along with the rest of Louise's herd. Following the Revolution, the Revolutionary Guard refused to allow his export to New Zealand on the grounds that the horse was a "plaything of the rich". Although attempts were made to remove Zeeland to the UK as a stepping stone to his new home, delicate negotiations were finally terminated when the New Zealand Embassy in Iran came under attack. Helen also tried to buy the foundation mare, Siyah Gosh*, from the UK but once again met with opposition - this time in the form of N.Z. import laws. She subsequently purchased stock imported by Australia from the UK.

The horses were kept at a seaside farm on the East coast at Matakana, near Warkworth, where Ana Rattray rode Atesh bareback along the beach, and in the sea, when she was only nine years old. All the imported stock were broken to ride (and some to drive) by Helen Rattray and her daughters.

Hopstone Atesh, an Arab-like chestnut stallion, out of Khorshid Kola* and by Karoun, was competed successfully by Ana and Victoria Rattray. He produced consistently good pure and part bred stock. In 1984 the New Zealand Horse Breeding Association approved Hopstone Atesh to stand at stud as a Riding Pony Stallion.

The first colt bred in New Zealand was Cheleken Avval Pesar (First son) by Atesh, out of the mare Every Lara.

Despite extensive T.V. coverage, especially in the early days, there are no other studs in New Zealand; however, part-bred Caspians have made a strong impact on the competition scene with a succession of top quality show and performance animals.

Helen designed a 'covering crate' to enable Atesh to cover mares of 15 hands and over. By crossing Hopstone Atesh with thoroughbred and Anglo Arab mares, then similarly re-crossing the offspring, she has produced a string of highly successful multi-purpose stock of between 13.2 hh and 16 hh. Most of these were taken to competition level by Ana and Victoria before being sold on to compete at higher level in showing, jumping and cross country and, in 1997, Atesh won the coveted Progeny Award for Hunter ponies, in New Zealand.

In 1984 Helen purchased Hopstone Tochal from Western Australia. In the same year violent storms killed her imported UK mare Hopstone Qahve (Maroun x Touran). Luckily, Helen had bred two fillies out of Qahve ('coffee'), as the Touran line is sparsely represented in the UK. Hopstone Tochal died in 1994.

Up to 1999, the stud bred 28 pure Caspians, several of which were exported to Australia. A mare, Cheleken Katushka, was exported to Japan and two mares were exported to Jordan.

In 1995 Cheleken Zemestani (1987) a mare by Hopstone Tochal, out of Cheleken Shamara (by Atesh) and a 1993 filly, Cheleken Kizzy Kola (by Atesh out of a mare by Tochal) were sold to Joyce and Felix Covington (MCC Farms) USA.

FRANCE/BELGIUM
Jean Michel Sourdin

The stallion Eastern Kashim Khan (Hopstone Jamshyd x Kineton Ismalla) and the filly Hopstone Bahar (Stesalwick Atilla - Hopstone Mustapha x Kineton Kistam - x Taliyeh) were exported to France from the UK. Kashim Khan was later gelded and Bahar was exported to Norway in 1998, for riding and breeding. UK owner/breeder Frances Smith-Boyes, moved to southern France with her four Caspian mares, including Ramesh and Hopstone Lili, and stallion, Costessa Siyroun. Hopstone Lili (Daria Nour* x Taloche*) and Costessa Siyroun (Karoun x Siyah Gosh*) are the sire and dam of Rosmear Kazem, shown at County level in ridden classes. His entire son was sold to Tina Staples in the USA early in 1996, followed by the mare, Hopstone Spark Ariana in 1998.

Early in 1995, Louise Firouz's daughter, Atossa, took the mare, Persicus Tehou ('Little Quail') and the stallion Persicus Amir, to Belgium. Both were from the 1994 Iran/UK importation.

USA/CANADA

Only one year after discovering her first Caspian, Louise Firouz sold a foundation stallion, Jehan* to Kathleen McCormick, a close friend of hers in Virginia. Louise had found Jehan* running wild in the mountains and kept him at Norouzabad for a year, during which time he was broken to ride and drive.

After walking to Teheran airport, up the marble steps into the terminal, Jehan* was loaded into a specially designed shipping crate and flown to New York via Lebanon, Cyprus, Italy, Switzerland and England. He arrived in New York four days later, on April 15th 1966 and quarantined for 60 days in New Jersey. On the day that Kathleen collected him, her station wagon and trailer were stuck in a traffic jam which made her several hours late and when she finally arrived, 10 minutes after the quarantine station had closed, she found Jehan* tied to a tree outside the gates. On the homeward journey her lights failed and they finished the last 300 miles of an 8,000 mile journey by tying torches to the front of the vehicle with the laces from a pair of tennis shoes!

Jehan* took part in a Bicentennial celebration at the Washington International Horse Show. He was invited to appear again two years later and he also represented the breed at Lexington, Kentucky, at the World Championship Three Day Event.

Kathleen formed the North American Caspian Society in 1966 and Jehan* began his showing career in 1967, never being 'out of the ribbons'.

Kathleen had been shown photographs of Louise's Caspians in Iran and picked Jehan* out of the group for his:

"overall correct conformation, outstanding top line, exquisite "classic" head and his exceptional size (12 hands - which was rare in Iran). There was then and is now a very limited market on the east coast for small ponies (up to 12.2). This made it of paramount importance that our Caspian 'pony' be as large as possible to encourage breeders of crossbred show hunter ponies .... For many years pony breeders would visit the farm and say that the Caspian was exceptional in conformation and movement, spectacular even, but they just didn't want to take the chance of breeding another small pony (12.2. and under). Jehan* was a viable breeding stallion until he was 29 years old. It was mainly North American Caspian Society members who used Jehan*, to improve their breeding programs. It was only the last few years of his life that breeders finally began to understand the important aspects of this ancient breed and the contribution the Caspian could make to cross bred breeding programs."

Despite the success of Jehan and his offspring Kathleen rarely referred to the possible connection between the Caspian and the Arab horse, since the general US horse market, at that time, was greatly prejudiced against the Arab.
Although he had no pure bred offspring, Jehan* sired a number of very successful cross bred Hunter ponies in the U.S., none of which have ever been sold on by their breeders. The only pure Caspian, sired by Jehan*, the stallion Jehangir, died in Iran without procuring the line.
His son, Jehad, a liver chestnut part-bred Welsh, is used as a Hunter pony stallion and stands at stud with Kathleen. Jehan* died in December 1993.
In 1973 a grey stallion, Mehregan, (Ostad* x Mehri*) was exported to Dr. Samuel Ross of Green Chimneys School, Brewster, Long Island (New York) direct from Iran. Mehregan did not have access to pure-bred mares and was leased to Jon and Cathy Johnson in Virginia in 1988 where he took part in the Washington County Parade of Breeds. He was later leased to ProtoArabians in 1994. ProtoArabians, who imported stock from the UK and Australia in 1994/95, made strenuous efforts to trace and reclaim the bloodlines of the Caspians previously imported. Sadly Mehregan died shortly afterwards without siring any stock.
In 1975 the grey foundation mare, Nourie*, was exported to Venezuela from Iran by Mr. Hassan Nemazee. Unfortunately Proto-Arabians were unable to trace Nourie who would then in any event have been 22 years old.
Kineton Khamyab (Maroun x Fatemeh*), a mare bred by Mrs. Suzanne Dore, was exported from the UK to the Vaughan family in Toronto, Canada in 1981 and remains there, never having been bred to a Caspian. An attempt by ProtoArabians to purchase the mare was unsuccessful and the combination of distance and age proved too great for a mating to take place with one their stallions. As Fatemeh* has only one surviving daughter in the UK, Khamyab would have been a valuable addition.
An unsuccessful attempt was made by Dr. Peter Neufeld at Minnedosa to export a part bred Caspian filly (x Welsh) bred by Suzanne Dore, in order to refine the Canadian Rustic Pony, which he had bred by crossing the Tarpan with Canadian mares.
It also proved impossible to import further mature stock into Canada when a ban was imposed in order to protect their stock against equine diseases. Youngstock, under two

New Zealand - exported stallion, Hopstone Atesh. (Karoun x Khorshid Kola*) Atesh is a highly successful competition stallion and winner of the 1997 Progeny Award as sire of hunter ponies in New Zealand.

Hopstone Bahar - exported to France in 1987 - a ride and drive mare from the rare Fatemeh* line. She was exported to Norway in 1998 and her first foal is expected in 1999.

years old, were not included in the ban. However, attempts to import foals into Canada were also frustrated by Canadian importation laws when an outbreak of equine metritis hit Newmarket.

Sadly no further stock was exported to facilitate the breeding of pure Caspians in the USA until April 1994 when ProtoArabians imported seven Caspians from the UK, followed by further importations, mostly under two years of age. These were joined by stock (including some older animals) from Australia and New Zealand, purchased by Joyce and Felix Covington and ProtoArabian Horses.

A further shipment to Joyce and Felix Covington, Mrs. Jane Macon and Mrs. Harlan left the Henden Stud in December 1995, which included youngstock bred from the 1994 Iranian imports to the UK, Persicus Nicky, Persicus Amir and Persicus Ai Banou. In all, 50 pure bred Caspians were imported by the USA during 1994 and 1995. The 1994 shipment (by ProtoArabians) consisted of the stallions Kineton Khalif and Runnymede Karamat and the mares, Shepton Tarraneh, Runnymede Karouna, Runnymede Iris, Mullacot Bathsheba, Runnymede Beryl and Henden Shazee.

Exports to the USA from Australia, by Joyce & Felix Covington, included three stallions and five mares bred by Chippendale and Marida Studs. Two mares were purchased from New Zealand. ProtoArabian Horses purchased eight mares from Western Australia, all but one of which were bred by Tandara Stud.

Importations by the USA from all Caspian breeding countries has re-united bloodlines which have narrowed in individual countries (e.g. Anahita*) and which can hopefully be strengthened by their re-union in the USA.

The Caspian Horse Society of the Americas

In 1994, The Caspian Horse Society of the Americas was founded by Mr. Patrick Carmack, Sister Angela Chandler, Mrs. Patricia Love and Mr. John Garza, who were the four Directors of the Society. Louise Firouz was declared an Honorary Director and Honorary Founder Member. Elwyn Hartley Edwards, Equine Historian, and Dr. E. Gus Cothran of the Department of Veterinary Science, Kentucky University, also became Honorary Directors.

Studs

Up to January 1996 there were eight owners/breeders of pure bred stock in the USA.

Proto-Arabian Horses, LLC

Brenham - Texas

Proto-Arabian Horses LLC were founded at the Monastery of St. Clare, Brenham, Texas USA., situated roughly half way between Waco and Houston. It was established in 1994 by the four American miniature horse owners, Mr. Patrick Carmack, Sister Angela Chandler, Mrs. Patricia Love and Mr. John Garza, who also founded the Caspian Horse Society of the Americas.

Having read about the Caspian breed in The Ultimate Horse Book (Elwyn Hartley Edwards) in February 1994, they commenced an abortive search for Caspians in the USA, which led them ultimately to Muriel and Rosemary Harris in the UK. Alan and Nadia Whitley, of the St. Giles Caspian Stud in Berkshire, UK, undertook the mammoth task of tracking down Caspians for sale, under the age of two years, arranging inspections, stabling and isolation, and surmounting the mounds of 'red tape' which the Caspian Stud UK had encountered almost two decades before on the inward journey. Two Caspians out of the first shipment had to be substituted at the last moment, with Alan and Nadia having to re-arrange all the relevant inspections and tests.

The Monastery of St. Clare, is the home of the Poor Clare Order, founded by St. Francis and St. Clare in the thirteenth century. Originally, it was composed of Cuban refugee nuns who fled Cuba after Castro's revolutionaries took over their monastery in Havana. John Garza began his association with the Monastery as a child visitor and then as a horse trainer and consultant to the stud which the nuns ran as a means of support, under the name, 'Monastery Miniatures'. Patricia Love and Patrick and Elizabeth Carmack purchased miniature horses from the Monastery and became friendly with John Garza and Sister Angela Chandler, Mother Superior. ProtoArabians was sold in 1997 to Anne and Les Stevens, who moved the stock to new premises at Texana Farms, Waller, Texas, and have been responsible for many more shipments from the UK.

MCC Farms, Brenham, Texas
Joyce & Felix Covington
MCC Farms is a miniature horse stud owned by Joyce and Felix Covington of Brenham, Texas. Shortly after the first shipment of Caspians to ProtoArabian Horses, Joyce & Felix Covington had occasion to visit Australia on a business trip. By chance, they were told of miniature horses nearby and the result was the purchase of seven Caspian mares and three stallions from New Zealand and South Australia. These were followed by two colts and two fillies from the Henden Caspian Stud, U.K in December 1995.

> "We began our journey to secure several of the Caspians in order to preserve an endangered species. In turn, we found the Caspian exemplifies the beauty, curiosity, friendly nature and picturesque gait that was described to us by those who owned these wonderful horses. The Caspian is everything we had hoped for and more ..... ".
>
> Joyce Covington

They are now committed to the survival of the breed and it is their intention to breed only pure-breds. Their first foal and the first Caspian to be born on American soil, arrived in October 1995. The foal, appropriately named MCCs Americas Premier Laila is out of Marida Jostan, who was bred to the stallion Marida Hushang before leaving Australia. They have since purchased many more Caspians from the UK and Australasia.

The following studs purchased stock from the first two shipments to the USA:
Southwest Caspians, Oklahoma City
James Russ
purchased Costessa Bellamira and Mullacot Chestnut
Imperial Caspians
Sister Theresa Harrison
Imperial Caspians are located at a Carmelite Monastery in Gallup, New Mexico.
They purchased Henden Sonata, St. Giles Scherezade and Mote Shalaby
Mar-Jacs Miniatures, Conroe, TX
Mr. & Mrs. J. Wood

purchased Henden Phillipa
Alpha & Omega Caspians, Houston TX
Mrs. Patricia A. Love
purchased Henden Shazee and Runnymede Camelia
Mrs. Jane Macon
Mrs. Harlan
imported Henden Stock in December 1995 and subsequent shipments
Mrs. Vicki Hudgins, Florida
purchased the first-shipment stallion, Kineton Khalif, and the mare, Mote Shallaby. She later imported Spark Azita.

಄಄

Runnymede Karamat - one of the stallions in the first shipment from the UK to the USA in 1994 (Karoun x Runnymede Penny Royal) bred by Rosemary Harris

First foal born in the USA (1995) MCC's Premier Laila by Marida Hushang Dam: Marida Jostan (exported in foal from Australia)

Anahita - dam of Pourandokht

Pourandokht – dam of the exported mare, Touran

The imported mare, Doueez.

Mehri – Dam of the imported stallion, Mehran

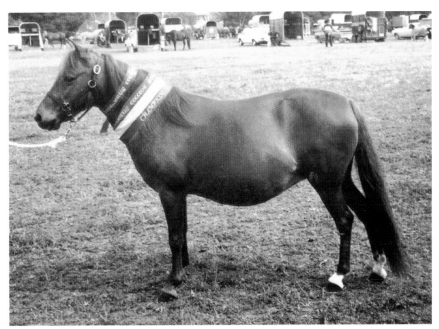

Marida Shereen (Karoun x Gulpar) - exported in utero from the UK to South Australia
(owned by the Marida Stud, established by Ida Graham and Marshall Steer)

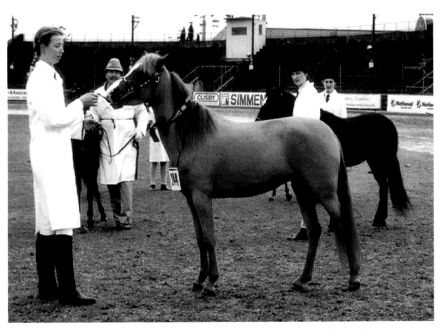

Marida Tarikh - pure bred Caspian - embryo transfer (Marida Hushang x
Marida Shereen) - using a Clydesdale mare

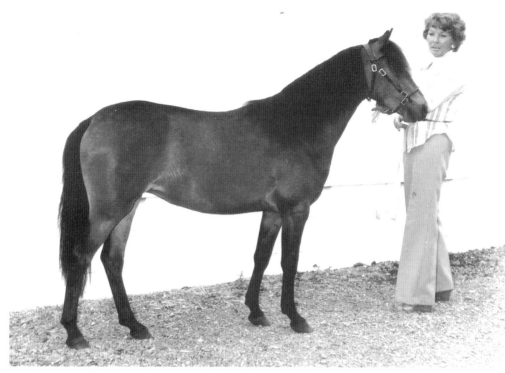

Hopstone Lili (Daria Nour* x Taloche*) exhibited by 'Jaffa' Jenvey at the Royal Agricultural Show, Stoneleigh. Owned by Fran Smith-Boyes in France, Lili is an exceptional jumper.
(Courtesy of Farmers Guardian)

Stallion, Jehan* - the first caspian registered in the International Stud Book and the first Caspian exported from Iran (USA)   (Courtesy of Pat MacVeagh)

CHAPTER SEVEN
ESTABLISHMENT OF A BREED SOCIETY IN THE UK

The first British Caspian Society was formed by Liz Alderson in 1975. At that time Liz and her partners, "Jaffa" Jenvey and "Griff" Griffin, owned most of the stock in the UK. For the next seven years Liz wrote and produced detailed newsletters, in which she logged matings, foalings, sales and deaths relating to early imports and foundation stock, along with the everyday running of the Caspian Stud UK. Strongly supported by her partners, she took over the registration of all stock from the former Iranian Royal Horse Society, organised shows, exhibitions, publicity, and sponsorship, along with overseeing the prolonged and diplomatically demanding arrangements for the various importations.

By 1980 the needs of the horses had outgrown the Society and a charitable Trust was set up with three members acting as Trustees. Vice Presidents of the Trust were the (then) Crown Equery, Lt. Col. Sir John Miller, Louise Firouz and Mr. Arthur Griffin. In 1986 the Trust reverted to the title British Caspian Society, with a Council of Management in order to meet the needs of a larger membership and to shoulder the growing mountain of work which fell on so few people. As the Society were responsible for the preservation and management of a rare breed, the duties of Council were more diverse than that of an established breed. Teething troubles were inevitable and the Society split into two separate groups. This proved to be undesirable for the breed, which then also had two separate registers, and members were re-united in 1989 under the name and constitution of the Caspian Pony Society, renamed Caspian Horse Society (CHS) in 1998, which is now the official Breed Society.

The Caspian Horse Society and Stud Book
The Caspian Horse Society are considered to hold the 'mother' Stud Book.
The logo adopted by The Caspian Horse Society is based on the 'Caspian' horses from the procession of gift bearers at the Palace of Persepolis.

The role of the Society in the Preservation of the Caspian
Since 1976, when the Ministry of Agriculture, Fisheries and Food handed over responsibility for the licensing of stallions to their own respective breed Societies, the Society has licensed it's own stallions. The first licensing scheme was improvised to balance the importance of maintaining bloodlines with the equally important need to maintain standards so that congenital faults would not be passed on to the detriment of the breed. Therefore, the first generation of stallions born in the UK were accepted provided that they were of Caspian type and had no genetic defects.

A panel of Inspectors was chosen, headed by the Registrar, then Liz Alderson. In order to ensure that all Inspectors used the same standard of consistency, a Judges Seminar was arranged at the Eastern Stud, Warwickshire, home of Jennifer and Robin Quinney.

When the next generation of stallions were available for breeding, a Veterinary Inspection replaced the panel of Inspectors in order to introduce a more stringent standard to the licensing of stallions. The Society also became a member of the National Stallion Association (NASTA).

A grading-up procedure was set in place by the first British Caspian Society as a safeguard against the problems which could have arisen in the event of in-breeding. Sensible breeding policies ensured that its use was unnecessary and this was discarded in 1998.

In 1985 a Performance Incentive Project was established by Eric Worthington, a former Chef D'Equipe for the BSPS and a well known judge of Working Hunter Ponies. Eric also served as a member of Council and became a life member of the Society in 1978. He was also an Inspector on the Stallion Licensing Panel. The Performance Incentive Project was intended to conform to the Stallion Performance Scheme which may at some time in the future be required by NASTA. At that time, the stallions Rostam, Maroun, Middleton Shir, Hopstone Mustapha, Mehran, Hopstone Shabdiz and Hopstone Jamshyd were all capable of the set standards. Unfortunately this Project was 'lost' in the change-over of Societies.

The Society is also represented on the Horse and Pony Breeds Committee of the British Horse Society and is affiliated to the Central Prefix Register.

The Caspian stand at the Royal Show, Warwickshire, was effective in introducing the Caspian to the UK and approximately half of the early Caspian studs were formed following a visit to the stand, which was organised and usually tended by Liz, Jaffa, volunteer members of the Society. Imported stallions, Mehran and Maroun, were two of the earlier Caspians to appear on the stand. Maroun also appeared in harness. Sponsorship from Arthur Griffin's Dart Spring Co. and a top Lancashire show hunter pony owner enabled the Society to run the stand for 19 years.

Although Caspian classes were held over the years at joint venues, such as Yelverton, in 1985 the first Annual Caspian Breed Show in its own right was held at the home of the Henden Caspian Stud, Ide Hill, Sevenoaks, Kent.

The following year, a Breed Show was established by Liz Alderson, with the assistance of Jennifer Quinney and Pandora Rene, at the Royal Agricultural Showground at Stoneleigh in Warwickshire.

Despite the rarity of the breed, entries came from as far afield as Ross-shire in northern Scotland, Kent, Lincoln and France. Fifteen owners exhibited three times as many ponies, ridden by small children in mixed classes of stallions and mares. As well as the usual in-hand classes there were jumping and Ride and Drive classes. Concours d'elegance and two small children 'borrowed' Caspians for the gymkhana, having never ridden them before - one was the stallion, Mustapha.

An attempt to cut costs was made in 1991, when the show was moved to Markfield Equestrian Centre, near Leicestershire and the following year the event was held at the home of Alan and Nadia Whitley, at Chalfont St. Giles, being closer to the nucleus of Caspians in the UK. However members living in the north felt that it was necessary to find a more central venue.

At the invitation of Col. Sir John Miller, the 1996 Breed Show was held at Windsor and was attended by H.M. The Queen, who presented the Champion and Reserve Champion Awards respectively to the stallion Hopstone Shabdiz and the mare Achnaha Klio, who had her first foal at foot. Both are out of HRH Prince Philip's mare, Khorshid Kola*. In 1998 Hopstone Shabdiz was chosen to represent the Caspian as one of the four original horse types, at the Festival of the Horse at Ascot.

In 1991, the CHS was invited to select a stallion to exhibit at the Burghley Horse Trials when Pandora Rene's stallion, Sunbeam Tarminh, was chosen to represent the breed. Although regularly ridden and shown, ironically, Tarminh (who was the only stallion out of the mare Touran), remained unused up to his tragic death in 1995, mainly due to his comparative

HM The Queen, Col. Sir John Miller and Ron Scott (left) of the Henden Stud. Her Majesty presented the Championship trophy at the Caspian Horse Society Breed Show at Windsor (1996). Supreme Ch. Hopstone Shabdiz and Res. Achnaha Klio (shown here) were both out of HRH Prince Philip's mare, Khorshid Kola* (Courtesy of Ann Priest)

Rostam (offside) and Maroun at Smiths Lawn, Windsor - 1978   Driven by Head Coachman, Mr. Ernest Long   (photo: S. Lemoine)

Veteran, Hopstone Shabdiz - at 18 years - (Palang* x Khorshid Kola*) Shabdiz was Breed
Champion in 1996   (photo: Brenda Dalton)

Achnaha Klio, the last foal out of Khorshid Kola*. Klio was Res. Ch. at the 1996 Caspian Breed Show
and Supreme Champion in 1997. Her full sister, also owned by Barbara Smathers, is six inches taller.

72

isolation on the Isle of Anglesey, North Wales.

CHS stallions and foundation stock are blood-typed on a voluntary basis, for which a £10 subsidy has been available. It is likely that, at some stage, the blood typing of all breeding stock will become compulsory.

Although the Caspian Horse Society has a membership of less than 200, this figure grows with Caspian ownership, which until recently has been frustrated by the low numbers of pure bred Caspians available for sale.

The British Caspian Stud Book was opened in 1976. Only stock originating from Foundation Caspians are eligible for registration.

Each owner of a licensed stallion is issued with a set of numbered documents, allocated to that stallion and recorded. One form is completed by the stallion owner for each mare covered and the top section retained for eventual return to the Registrar as the stallion return. The bottom section becomes both covering certificate and foal registration document as it carries both the details of the covering and space for the mare owner to record the details of the resulting foal (including full physical identification). The number is stamped on both portions so that when the Registrar receives the Application for Foal Registration, she can marry it up with the stallion return and number originally allotted to that stallion as an additional security check.

With effect from 1st January 1996 only stock (pure bred and part bred) under 18 months of age is eligible for registration in the CHS Register. There are no retrospective registrations or stallion licences.

Part-bred Stud Book

Caspian stallions have been crossed with a variety of native, Arab and (in New Zealand) TB mares. These crosses are recorded in Part-bred Stud Books.

Societies and/or Registers also exist in Iran, North America, Western Australia, Australasia, New Zealand, the Americas and Scandinavia.

THE INTERNATIONAL CASPIAN SOCIETY AND STUD BOOK

THE INTERNATIONAL CASPIAN STUD BOOK

The International Caspian Stud Book was established in 1978 as a medium for recording the progress of the Caspian as a rare breed, around the world.

THE INTERNATIONAL CASPIAN SOCIETY

The International Caspian Society was formed In 1995, following the importation of stock into the USA, the founder members being the Societies or Registers in Iran, the UK, South Australia, Western Australia, New Zealand and the U.S.A.. The International Caspian Stud Book has now been incorporated into the International Caspian Society and is responsible for the co-ordination of information and stock registered with Breed Societies or Registers throughout the world. One member of each Society or Register (usually the Registrar), provides details of all registered stock to the International Registrar.

The International Caspian Society will only register Iranian foundation stock and stock, under two years of age, which originate from Iranian foundation stock and are the produce of licensed stallions.

The Society is also responsible for providing statistics annually to Rare Breeds International.

Member Societies are required to supply details of :

1. Stock registered throughout the year
2. Stallions licensed
3. Transfers and deaths
4. New studs established
5. Imports and exports

Member Societies are also required to conform with ICS rules and standards.

ଛଠ

CHAPTER EIGHT
CHARACTERISTICS AND USE

Description and Similarities with the Arab Horse

The main colours of the breed are bay, grey, roan or chestnut, with the occasional black, dun or cream. Registered pure breds have ranged from less than 9 hands to over 13 hands in height (the original Achamaenian miniature horse probably stood no more than 9 hands) The Caspian should be of narrow build, although the richer feed available to them in the UK means that few Caspians bred outside Iran, and turned out to grass, have quite the same 'lean' shape as their Iranian cousins.

The coat is fine, often with an iridescent sheen. A large number of Caspians, including bays and greys, carry a dorsal stripe which sometimes crosses at the wither. Some also display 'zebra' striping across the backs of the forelegs. One imported Caspian stallion is known to carry the gene which creates the 'mealy' muzzle present in the Exmoor pony.

In winter the coat of the Iranian Caspian is often dense (not coarse) with a velvet texture. Whilst most Caspians are able to winter out, with a field shelter and/or New Zealand rug, not all Caspians in the UK grow thick coats and these need to be treated in the same manner as a 'blood' horse. Most seem to be able to weather extreme cold but they do not do well in continual wet conditions.

The typical Caspian head should be short and fine with large eyes, set wide apart. The vaulted shape which is so prominent in the foals is rarely pronounced in the adult horse. The variations which appear in the Arabian breeds are inclined to appear in the Caspian. The width across the forehead varies. Although most have narrow heads, some have the broad forehead of the Barb. Viewed from the side, the head is usually straight, apart from a slight vaulting above the eyes. The nasal bone is either straight or slightly concave, although some have a slight rounding of the nasal bone (usually from the stallion Palang), which should still possess quality. The Caspian should have a small muzzle, large nostrils and small in-pricked ears.

Whilst the Breed Standard specifies a graceful neck, there is sometimes a strengthening of the muscle under the neck, similar to that of the procession horses at Persepolis. No doubt this strength was an asset to the carriage horses of Darius. Although most Caspians have a fine, silky mane and tail, the manes and tails of stallions (and some mares) can be quite prolific (again, as in the Barb). The Caspian more closely resembles the Shagya Arab than any other - elegant, dainty, with natural balance and paces, and is very similar to ride.

The great intelligence and ability to think, which is attributed to the Arab, and the docility which is linked particularly with the Shagya Arab, is also intense in the Caspian, coupled with boldness, great curiosity and a love of people. They are extraordinarily friendly. A house door left open will usually attract a Caspian. The Caspian will actively seek eye contact with people and the attitude of the Caspian towards his owner is often described as "doglike", a characteristic which is also attributed to the Arabian horse. Despite the biddable temperament of the breed, it should be remembered that, like the Arab, the Caspian is a hot blood and management of youngsters, in particular, should be overseen by knowedgeable persons.

The looks, spirit, freedom of movement, intelligence and temperament of the majority of Caspians, make them extremely versatile. Despite the comparatively short time that they have been competing in the UK there is already no field untrodden by the Caspian. Driving events, gymkhana, lead-rein, first ridden, dressage, jumping, cross country and in-hand classes have all had winners from the small pool of available Caspians.

Originating in the mountains, the Caspian can be almost deer-like at scrambling between rocks and browsing amongst sparse shrubbery. Most Caspians prefer to forage for greenery than to eat hay supplied in the field.

Many Caspian breeders have commented on the preference shown by the Caspian for their own kind. Caspians turned out in a field will usually team up with other Caspians and often show only initial regard for other breeds in neighbouring fields. Caspian stallions exhibit a preference for Caspian mares which, if this is true of Caspians in the wild, could account in part for the preservation of breed 'type' over the 'lost' years. The Caspian is usually a very active little horse and is happier working, even when undertaking stud duties.

The hoof is strong, small and oval shaped and, in Iran, only needs to be shod on the roughest terrain. However, UK breeders find that for repeated road work, shoes are not only advisable but necessary. The words "Only requires shoeing on the very roughest ground" have now been removed from the original Breed Standard as they were taken too literally by some owners.

The Caspian has a long walk, natural far reaching action at the trot, a smooth, comfortable canter, and is capable of keeping up with a normal horse at all gaits except rapid gallop. His length of stride is slightly longer than that of a pony of equal size. His jumping ability is extraordinary and most Caspians are capable of jumping courses set for much larger animals, if riders can be found for them. The long, low stride allows the sitting trot to be ridden smoothly.

As well as being the ideal mount for children, an average sized adult riding one of the larger Caspians is often surprised at the experience.

Horse or pony?

The Caspian has the bone structure, symmetry and demeanor of a well-proportioned miniature horse. Without the inclusion of a person to add perspective, a photograph of a Caspian can give the illusion of a thoroughbred, Anglo Arab or Arab horse of 14.2 hands or more. Yet, because of its size, is the Caspian a pony? This subject has been the cause of bitter argument, both within the Breed Society and outside.

Another subject which has attracted a great amount of debate is that of 'type'. There is, as was mentioned in Chapter One, a variation within the breed which has been the basis of much discussion and controversy. Although there are valid arguments for maintaining 'true Caspian type', it is still too early in the preservation of the breed to risk losing genes, particularly when the different types can be produced from the same parents.

Some owners argue that the breed resembles the thoroughbred and not the Arab, as originally suggested; others, that the average Caspian is more akin to the Anglo-Arab or the Turkoman.

With a difference of 4 hands between the smallest and the largest Caspians, in all probability, there will come a time when a line will have to be drawn between the dainty, delicate type of Caspian and the stronger, taller (though no less refined) type of Caspian. Perhaps, at some time in the future, either a grading system or a 'Section' system (perhaps similar to that in the Welsh breed) may have to be introduced. However, it was decided by the Caspian Horse

Society, in 1992, that it was then still too early in the breeding programme to risk narrowing the genetic base by setting preferences for a particular type.

The height factor cannot simply be explained by better husbandry or feeding, since animals with the same parentage, and under the same management, can produce extremes in size. An example of this are the last two foals born to the foundation mare Khorshid Kola*, full sisters, Achnaha Kinnara and Achnaha Klio, by Costessa Al Mutakabir, which vary in height by almost two hands. Without losing any of the usual quality produced by Khorshid Kola*, Kinnara is one of the largest Caspians bred, at over 13 hands, whilst Klio, Supreme Champion at the 1997 Caspian Breed Show, is a dainty perfect miniature thoroughbred-type of 11.2 hands. Costessa Mutakabir was one of the larger stallions, out of the foundation mare, Siyah Gosh*, and by the imported stallion, Mehran (Aseman* x Mehri*). Whilst it would appear that Siyah Gosh* produced the height, she also produced Hopstone Shoja (by Maroun) senior stallion at the Henden Stud, who is very much valued for his small size, as well as his impeccable temperament!

Whilst Achnaha Klio is undoubtedly more Caspian in 'type', Kinnara is a superb quality riding horse, possessing genes which should not be lost to the breed, which could happen if a height limit were to be introduced. It is also quite possible that Kinnara herself could produce small foals. As Costessa Al Mutakabir was gelded having sired only these two mares, there are strong reasons for maintaining his genes through both mares, since he is an all-round performance horse of some merit. As well as being broken to ride and drive, Mutakabir competes successfully at dressage and cross country events.

Whilst some owner/breeders have a preference for the small delicate type of Caspian, there are also owners/breeders who feel that without the larger Caspians the breed cannot forge a place for itself in the performance world.

Obviously, it is difficult for the types to be judged together and, if and when, more of the larger type are produced, provision may have to be made for their different attributes to be judged fairly.

A letter to the Registrar of the ICSB from Tony Gyles in Western Australia refers to size and type :

"I would quote from our judges ...."Judges have to be very careful that they do not change a breed by rewarding those animals that concur with their own preferences rather than with the breed standard of excellence". "May I remind you all that you are now in a position in W.A. to change the Caspian species to what you think it should be rather than that which has been re-discovered, after nearly a thousand years of believed extinction. Note I say 'species' for with the stallions Amu Daria and Ruba (11) only one generation and the stallions Tochal and Kaftar only two generations descended from the original foundation stock we, homo sapiens, have not yet really had time to mess things up.

....due to good feeding 13 hands has already been reached in the UK whilst in South Australia things seem to have gone the other way with one at 8.2 hands (throw back in time, indiscriminate breeding or deliberate breeding using nothing but the smaller Tochal type?)

...... In the beginning the horse was, as you know, very small - eventually evolving to a small species for the hot climes and a larger one for the cold. In the Caspian my preference is for the small fine animal of the Tochal type but without the poor rump!

I believe this to be the truer historical horse. Kaftar" - owned by Tony and Betty Gyles - "was purchased sight unseen _ as being of suitable genes to stand over all the Caspian mares then known in Australasia. ... In view of the recent trends in judging Caspian classes it would seem timely that we revise our very old set of guidelines for judges, making them more concise and based mainly on the standard of excellence. I would also propose that they should end with the following paragraph:

"Within the Caspian breed there are three distinct types, each still retaining all the true Caspian characteristics. There is the small dainty fairy like animal generally around 10.1hh, then comes a slightly taller animal probably around 11.2 with a very proud carriage and lastly the heavier more workmanlike animal of about 12hh. This is fortunate inasmuch as it gives judges a chance to exercise their personal preference without detriment to the breed standard and means that the same animal is not winning all the time."

Differences between UK and Iranian Caspians

Caspians bred in England have changed very little from the original breeding stock.

Whilst some breeders claim that conformation has improved with better feeding and management in the UK, others are concerned about the temptation to 'westernise' the Caspian thereby losing the unique features of the breed.

In the UK they tend to grow slightly larger. The frog is more accentuated. They react well to cold, although not always to wet, conditions. The foundation animals in particular do not thrive in constant wet conditions, though subsequent generations are less affected. Management of the breed is still very much experimental due to the comparatively recent rediscovery of the Caspian and the change in environment.

Some complaints now occur which are common to the UK but which did not occur in Iran, e.g. sweet itch, laminitis and splints. However, some imported problems have been almost eliminated in the UK. Youngstock are often prone to "tooth bumps", although these usually disappear fairly quickly.

It is quite possible that some in-breeding occurred prior to the re-discovery of the foundation lines, causing problems which the Iranian and UK breeding policies have sought to eliminate, such as 'undershot jaw' and the early tendency towards cow hocks. However, in the case of foundation stock, the latter could also have been an after-effect of the hard work to which the little animals were submitted from a very early age, often over mountainous or swampy terrain.

An occasional incidence of slightly wide action in the hind legs also appears occasionally in the Arab horse, where it is thought to be an indication of desert breeding, as is the once acclaimed ability to 'pace', which was more comfortable for the stirrupless riders of the distant past:

"He rode a white Turkoman horse .... Its favourite pace was a peculiar amble or run which Turkomans teach their horses and which is performed with its hind legs very wide apart. The Persians look upon this idiosyncrasy as a good sign in a horse"

Curzon's Persia   G.N. Curzon   Sidgewick and Jackson

Several Caspians are known to pace e.g. Christine Belton's tandem wheeler, Hopstone Chahar Shambe.

The Iranian Caspians at first bred only bi-annually but were later given mineral supplements and hormone treatment. This problem does not occur in the U.K, any more than it does in other breeds, and it is now thought that it only occurred in Iran prior to purchase by Louise Firouz, where foals were left on the mares over winter and sometimes during the following spring. Louise also found that the first Caspians she bought were more inclined towards colic than other Iranian breeds, possibly due to worm damage in some of the foundation stock. Two of the imported mares, Touran and Shirine*, suffered stress colic in their early years in the UK - in Shirine's case this was almost certainly due to early worm damage. Great care was taken to eliminate stress from the lives of these two mares. With correct feeding and worming, this problem has also been reduced to normal levels in successive generations.

Care should be taken not to overfeed as most Caspians do well on sparse grazing but some are not particularly good doers and individual animals should be fed accordingly.

Similarities between the ancient and the modern Caspian

In comparison with other breeds, the head is narrower. The formation of the forehead consists of two parietal bones linked down the centre by the inter-parietal bone. According to Louise Firouz the elevation of the parietal and interparietal bones is more pronounced in the Caspian and the formation of the frontal bone is quite concave, unlike that of any other horse, except perhaps that of the Desert Arab and the Plateau Persian. It is sufficiently obvious to be observed in some live animals. This formation highlights a distinct diamond shape (known as the Jibbah in the Arab). The interparietal bone does not close to form a parietal crest as in other horses but continues unbroken to the back of the head.

PARIETAL STRUCTURE

This unique bone structure is also evident in the Lydian 'tribute' horses, marching their way along the walls of the ancient Palace of Persepolis. It appears in the tiny horses braving lions on the seal of Darius, those carrying Ardashir 1 to his Investiture; Shapur in defeat over Valerian and harnessed in gold as part of the Oxus treasure. All are waist high and have tiny ears, fine legs and a crested neck.

That the Caspian was trusted with the safety and reputation of the King during high speed lion hunts comes as no surprise to the owners of Caspians today. Invariably they recognise the boldness, obedience and athleticism displayed by their own animals.

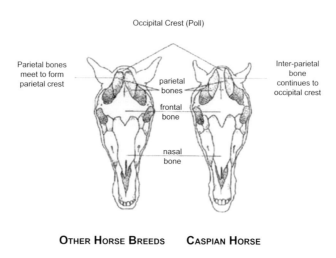

OTHER HORSE BREEDS   CASPIAN HORSE

Cyclic Crossing and Line Breeding

Following exportation to the UK in 1976, there were only four sire lines readily available to breeders outside Iran, where events ruled out the acquisition of further bloodlines. A carefully planned programme of cyclic crossing and line breeding in the UK was established to ensure as broad a genetic base as possible.

This programme, devised by Lawrence Alderson, Technical Consultant with the Rare Breeds Survival Trust, produced a minimum of inbreeding levels and was recently applauded by Gus Cothran of Kentucky University. Of necessity, less desirable genes were maintained along with the more desirable ones and only now, with the breed relatively safely established, can cautious action be taken in order to alleviate any flaws perpetuated this way.

The lack of stallion lines meant that foundation females were of equal importance. Whilst every effort was made to breed stallions from an equal number of female lines, stallion offspring from the mare Taliyeh far outweighed those from other founder mares. Because so many were available, and because Taliyeh consistently bred quality, it would have been very easy for stallions bred from Taliyeh to dominate the breed.

Wide, vaulted forehead - Ears are short, wide apart and often in-pricked. Mare - Spark Shirine Shara at three years.

Structure of the parietal bones (jibbah). Stallion - Runnymede Orion

A Turkoman mare owned by Louise Firouz. According to research by Kentucky University, the Turkoman holds an ancestral position with the Caspian Horse, the Caspian being the more primitive of the two.

81

For this reason it was necessary for mare owners to ignore personal preferences in stallion types in order to avoid in-breeding.

"In every breed there are fashionable sires and unfashionable sires. The former are over-subscribed and the latter are neglected, and this concentration of attention on a relatively small proportion of elite animals can lead to a loss of bloodlines and associated genetic material .... Thus in a numerically small breed there is a need for breeders to sacrifice some of their independence of action and participate in a broader breeding policy designed to safeguard the future interests of the breed as a whole .... The two basic principles of a group breeding policy are the maintenance of distinct bloodlines, and the use of cyclic crossing between these bloodlines to minimise the increase in the level of inbreeding. If those remnants of the Caspian breed, which may or may not exist still in Iran, are ignored, there are six extant sire lines in the breed on which to base a breeding programme.

"All the stallions and mares are allocated to one of these lines according to their type and the main influence in their pedigree. The best mares in each line are mated to stallions in the same line (line breeding) in order to maintain each line as a distinct entity. The other mares are mated to stallions in the next line in the cycle.

"The sequence of lines within the breed must be planned so that the weaknesses of a particular line are corrected by the strengths of the next line. This is known as compensatory mating."

Lawrence Alderson

Lawrence Alderson states that the typical pedigree of an animal bred in this way shows a coefficient of inbreeding of less than 1% in the first four generations.

Crossing lines and their influence on the present day Caspian

DARIA NOUR*

The Daria Nour* line is noted for jumping, small size, good head and forequarters but lacked good hocks and feet.

Daria Nour* has become extremely influential in the UK through his son, Forstals Barewa, out of the foundation mare, Pari*. Unfortunately, his progeny far exceeded that of all other stallions in the 1990's and care will need to be taken to ensure that this line does not overpower the breed in the next generation.

His progeny is dominant in Australia, via his son Amu Daria, out of the mare Mitra*.

PALANG*

In contrast the Palang* line had good hocks and conformation but had a less refined head and was taller than average.

Out of the twelve foals sired by Palang*, the line is mostly represented, in the UK, through his sons, Hopstone Shabdiz, out of the mare Khorshid Kola*, and Hopstone Jamshyd. Both stallions are Breed Champions.

RUBA*

The Ruba* line is of generally good type with a quality head and exceptional temperament.

Ruba* is strongly represented by Maroun, who has had significant influence on the breed through his twenty-six foals, including Hopstone Shoja. Ruba* is also well represented through Rostam, who sired seventeen foals including Karoun (also a well used sire), and the mares Hopstone Zardalu and Atesheh. Ruba's son (Ruba II) was also responsible for excellent stock.

Although the early influence of the Taliyeh and Ruba lines (Maroun, Karoun, Zardalu, Atesheh) at a time when so few Caspians existed, could have become a problem, careful outcrossing ensured that it did not.

Thus in the system of cyclic crossing, the best sequence for these three lines, according to Lawrence Alderson, was Daria Nour* > Palang* > Ruba*.

ASEMAN*
The Aseman* line, available only through the stallion Mehran, followed.
Although emphasis tends to be placed on the importance of male lines, in the case of the Caspian, female lines were of equal importance and the Aseman* line was available, minimally, through the 'in-utero' mares Winstay Roya and Kineton Kistam.

OSTAD*/FELFEL*
The Ostad* line was only available through the mare Taliyeh and the Bermudan mares, Momtaz-e-Mahal and Roshan. Felfel* was available only through the 'in-utero' mare Hopstone Banafsheh (Taliyeh).
Apart from a minimal degree of deliberate in-breeding by individual owners in order to 'set type', the policy of cyclic crossing and line breeding has avoided the problem of in-breeding and the breed has benefited greatly by the good sense of owners who have put the breed as a whole before their own personal preferences.

Eric Worthington, who was involved with the breed from its early days in the UK, and Gus Cothran (Kentucky University) have both expressed admiration for the achievements of UK breeders.

Cross Breeding
Glenda Spooner, in 'Riding' magazine, wrote:
"If you aim to breed a riding pony (other than one of the registered Native Breeds), especially a show specimen, then indeed you are fluke breeding. For every real show pony bred there must be thousands which for one reason or another fail to make the grade."
Most of these crosses were attemped using a small thoroughbred or small Arab on a native breed. Louise Firouz is convinced that use of the Caspian would take the guesswork out of breeding quality children's ponies with suitable temperaments.
In the UK, the Caspian has been bred to Shetlands, Welsh, Dartmoor and Arabs.
A pair of Welsh cross Caspians bred by Muriel Harris, have won almost every scurry driving event possible. Prester John, a larger part-bred from the Harris stable, was given a place in a team, which also included three Welsh Cobs, because, according to his trainer, he had "more brains than the rest of them put together".
In New Zealand, the Rattray family cross their Caspian stallions with either Arab or TB mares, then put the daughters of such matings to the outcross (Thoroughbred or Arab). The results, both half and quarter-breds, are exceptional both in looks and performance.

Influence of the Caspian on the modern horse

If the extensive research work towards proving that the Caspian is a proto-type of the Arab is accepted, then the historic Caspian has also influenced, in varying degrees, British native breeds such as the Welsh, the Connemara, the New Forest and (in lesser infusions) the Dartmoor and the Highland. Russia, Europe, Australia and America all have breeds which have been influenced by the Arab horse. The English Thoroughbred was established using three oriental stallions; the Byerley Turk (Turkoman) in the early 17th century, the Godolphin Arabian in the 1730's and the Darley Arabian in the early 19th century.

Some of the world famous Lipizzaner horses can be traced back to the Arabian stallion, Siglavy.

෪ාԲ

CHAPTER NINE
PERFORMANCE

The versatility of both pure and part-bred Caspians enables them to be used by any member of the family. In Iran, and in all the countries to which they have been exported, Caspians have proved their ability as useful, working animals; in the showring as lead rein, first ridden, ridden showing, working hunter and 'mountain and moorland' ponies. They are extremely competent in jumping and gymkhana classes, dressage, cross country and all driving events. In breed classes, the Caspian should be shown with manes and tails in a natural state.

IRAN
Louise Firouz used all her Caspians in the riding school near Teheran. She found them easy to tame and break and all, including her first find, Ostad*, demonstrated outstanding natural jumping ability and temperament.

Daria Nour* won almost every jumping event he entered and his son, Amu Daria inherited his staggering prowess over jumps.

In Iran, children as young as five years old raced stallions against each other and rode them in company with mares. They were regularly ridden out by the Firouz family on picnics.

Caspians which came to Louise following the Iran/Iraq war had been 'caught up' in a wide sweep of the mountains. Some were exceptionally wild, having fended for themselves for some months in huge dusty corrals amongst thousands of large wild horses. Even these quickly became tame after only a few weeks of human companionship at the Firouz farm.

USA
All stock in the USA prior to the 1994 importation was part bred by Jehan*. Born wild in the mountains of Iran, Jehan* was broken to ride and drive and was consistently "in the ribbons" in stallion classes.

His part-bred daughter Roshan, a 12.2 hands chestnut mare, was "3rd in the state of Virginia" in her third year, her major win being at an "A" show in Culpepper, Virginia. Jehan's daughters Setara Fair and Jemal-Amani, a 12.1 hands chestnut mare, are also successful show ponies.

U.K
Although there are few in-hand classes specifically for Caspians, some Riding Clubs and local shows allow entry into Mountain and Moorland classes. Shirley and Jeff Brailsford's stallion, Runnymede Orion, is regularly placed at a Lancashire Riding Club and local shows. Foreign Breeds shows are usually happy to accommodate the Caspian . and shows such as the Native Pony Performance Show at Alsager, Cheshire, provide separate classes for foreign breeds.

Of the foundation and imported stallions up to 1976, only Palang* was not broken to ride and drive due to his fear of being bridled, or even touched, when he first arrived in the UK. Mehran, Rostam, Maroun and Karoun were all broken to ride and drive.

Early public appearances and performance
As well as promotional appearances, in the early years, Liz Alderson and Jaffa Jenvey "criss-crossed" England with their transit horsebox competing with their Caspians.

The Caspian Stud UK strongly promoted the use of stallions and geldings in competition work. The Caspians were usually placed in the hands of top competitors. Daria Nour* (Dusty) was jumped by Tina Cassan, then a competent nine year old. His son, Darius, was broken to ride by Tina and her mother and was also jumped by Tina, who appeared on BBC television's Pebble Mill programme with him.

Darius was returned to Claverley for Liz Alderson's daughters to ride before moving on to Suzanne Dore, where, at 10.3 hands, and piloted by Suzanne's small nephew, he completed a show jumping course set for ponies of 14.2 hands. Under the watchful eye of Suzanne, they gave a showjumping display at the Queen's Silver Jubilee, City of Worcester Show.

The stallion, Maroun, was sent to Ron Elliott, (trainer of the Whitbread horses) where he was broken to a trap. After only one week he appeared on Pebble Mill TV with Daria Nour* and Tina Cassan. The following year he fearlessly steered the trap through the milling throngs at The Royal Show. On June 5th, 1977, Maroun appeared, in the company of a mare and foal, at the Queens Silver Jubilee, City of Worcester Show.

Elizabeth Gauvain paraded Prince Philip's stallion, Rostam, at the South of England Show the following week where Maroun was also driven in harness as a pair with his half brother, the stallion Karoun.

Rostam was also broken to ride and drive and his talents were equally diverse. In his later years he was used by Riding for the Disabled alongside his stud duties at the Darkhorse Stud in Yorkshire. Rostam died in 1993.

Driven as a pair, Maroun and Rostam took part in a Parade of Foreign and Unusual Breeds, on the occasion of the Queens Cup, in the presence of H.M. The Queen on Smiths Lawn, Windsor. (1978). On this occasion they were driven by the Head Coachman at the Royal Mews, Mr. Ernest Long.

Karoun also took part in the parade, led in hand by Rosemary Harris, followed by Darius, ridden by eight year old Philip Pettigrew. Khorshid Kola* and Safiyeh (her 9 week old filly foal) were led by 'Jaffa' Jenvey and Liz Alderson. Hopstone Banafsheh, newly broken and still on a leading rein, also carried a small rider.

Liz was given the honour of introducing the Caspians and their handlers to Her Majesty the Queen, who commented that she had seen "quite a lot" of Maroun and Rostam, who had spent some time at the Royal Mews in preparation for the parade. The vehicle, loaned by the Queen, was a very smart navy blue and red miniature landau with a magnificent set of harness, perfectly fitted to the stallions, which had been presented to the Queen by one of the Worshipful Companies of London.

The stallions had been driven from the Mews to Smith's Lawn, Windsor, and back again. The previous evening Mr. Long had treated Liz and her mother to a drive round the grounds of Windsor Castle in order to check that the two stallions, which hadn't seen each other for over a month, would still co-operate well together. They covered several miles at a spanking trot (particularly when passing fields of mares) and then repeated the exercise for Elizabeth Gauvain and her husband, who at that time had the loan of Rostam.

Shortly afterwards Maroun and Rostam took part in the Royal Windsor Horse Show's Interbreeds Obstacle Driving Competition for Pairs, again driven by Mr. Ernest Long, who was "extremely flattering about the stallions".

Christine Dick was successful with a driving pair of Caspian stallions, whilst her sister, Mavis Clarke, was once in the unique position of having beaten Christine's famous shetlands, Pavlov and Peanuts, with stallions Maroun and Middleton Shir.

Mustapha and Chahar Shambe

Now retired from top competition, the grey stallion, Hopstone Mustapha (Amu Daria x Taliyeh) and tandem partner, Hopstone Chahar Shambe (gelding) competed successfully in countless driving events at top level with owner Christine Belton. Both ponies were bred by the Caspian Stud UK and over the years they have also been ridden and driven extensively by Christine's daughters. Hopstone Chahar Shambe is one of the slightly larger type of Caspian, whilst Mustapha is the willowy, delicate type. In his early driving days he was affectionately known as 'the Biafran Racehorse' or 'the ballerina'. Mustapha's temperament is impeccable and he is one of only a handful of stallions allowed to compete at Pony Club. He is also used by Riding for the Disabled.

Hopstone Chahar Shambe is out of the imported mare, Touran. As a stallion, he covered one mare before being gelded in order that he could be used to promote the breed as a show pony. Although Touran produced several good foals, her bloodline is now only sparsely represented and Chahar Shambe proved to be a considerable loss to the breed as a stallion.

At their first competition (for Chris as well as Mustapha) they finished fourth overall. He was second in the dressage at Lilford Park, despite losing marks for presentation (as the vehicle was too big). Balsaghar, her other grey Caspian stallion (now gelded), finished fifth in the dressage and second in the cone driving.

When he was first introduced to tandem driving Mustapha was teamed up with Hopstone Balsaghar only three weeks before an event at Atherstone. Despite a few minor setbacks the tandem team finished second in the dressage. Mustapha finished third on the cross country (without time faults) and fourth overall.

They competed successfully at Windsor, Holker Hall, Cirencester, Lowther, Osberton, the National Carriage Driving Championships at Harrogate and at Hoghton Towers, Lancashire. Prince Philip, who often competed at the same events, took a keen interest in their progress.

Chris discovered, with mixed feelings, that Chahar Shambe could 'pace'. Since it is so frowned upon in the dressage arena, Chris had no desire to encourage him, especially as Shambe was nowhere near as good at dressage as Mustapha. In desperation she taught him to pace only on command.

Eastern Stud

Owned by Mrs. Jennifer Quinney of the Eastern Stud, Redditch, Hopstone Jamshyd was regularly shown in harness and well placed at County Shows, including the Windsor Horse Show. Jamshyd, bred by the Caspian Stud UK, is by the foundation stallion Palang* and out of the mare Hopstone Zara (Ruba II x Khorshid Kola*). He was broken to harness by Gillian Walker who drove him during his first outing, the Royal International Horse Show, at Birmingham, in 1987, where he was driven into fifth place in the Concours d'elegance.

Both Hopstone Jamshyd and his female stable companian, Hopstone Phoebe, display the spectacular jump attributed to the Caspian. Jenny places great emphasis on performance and, apart from the older breeding stock, the majority of Jenny's Caspians are broken to ride and/or drive. The only problem she has is finding riders who aren't 'jumped off' by the height they jump. Hopstone Phoebe is regularly shown under saddle and was champion at the Caspian Breed Show whilst on loan to Kimberley Kemp, an eight year old suffering from cystic fibrosis, who also won the Young Handler Award. During the time that Phoebe was on loan to Kimberley she also qualified for the Ponies UK championships.

Hopstone Mustapha (right) and Hopstone Chahar Shambe - consistent winners at top level
in all spheres - owner Christine Belton   (Courtesy of Jim Moore)

Blue Cloud, Dartmoor x Caspian (by Amu Daria) is a consistently successful ride and drive mare.
Cloud, owned by Vicki Poole, can clear "anything under 4' 3" from a standstill.
(photo: Brenda Dalton)

Most Caspians are easy to break and owners are often surprised by the speed of their response. Khorshid Kola* was broken to harness at 22 in order to prevent her from becoming bored during retirement, following a lifetime of breeding. Her daughter, Atesheh, was broken to ride at eleven, having 'missed' a year following a succession of foals. Atesheh was on loan at the time to Olwen Brown in Yorkshire. Olwen's daughter, who expected it to take her approximately six weeks to break Atesheh, simply placed a saddle on her back and rode her away. Two years later, loaned to Suzanne Dore, Atesheh was back in foal and was ridden and bred successfully until her death in 1994.

Runnymede
A pair of Welsh cross Caspians bred by Muriel Harris have won almost every scurry driving event possible for owner Colin Cornwell. Prester John, a larger part-bred was included in a four-in-hand with three Welsh cobs. Runnymede Lalah (Tulip), a pure bred Caspian out of Hopstone Banafsheh (Felfel) bred by Muriel Harris, was pulled in eighth at her first show in a line up of twenty top class lead rein ponies.

Blue Cloud, a part bred Caspian (Amu Daria) x Dartmoor (Bluebell) owned by Mrs. Vicki Poole from Stourbridge made an immediate impact on the driving scene with five firsts, seven seconds, four thirds and four fourths. Vicky had hardly any driving experience when she broke Cloud to harness but "with the help of a good book and a friend, everything went quite smoothly". She describes Cloud as keen to do whatever she asks of her, very responsive, yet stands "as quietly as a mouse" as soon as she has finished, a real character and very intelligent. Although Vicky only uses her jumping prowess over low obstacles in ride and drive events, she says that the mare is able to simply 'rear' over any flat topped gate or stable door under 4ft 3ins which gets in her way.

In the UK two thirds of stallions are broken to saddle and/or harness and approximately one third are regularly shown either in Caspian classes or in competition with other breeds

At the 1993 Caspian Breed Show more than thirty children took part in the ridden classes, often on stallions, including Eloise Chouamider riding Eastern Kashim Khan (then a stallion), whose owners had made the trip back from France in order to compete.

NEW ZEALAND
The Rattray family in New Zealand, where the Caspian/Thoroughbred cross has been particularly successful, found that demand for the part bred sports horse far outweighed that for the pure bred Caspian. Over the years they have achieved an enviable chain of results from their home bred and home produced Caspians and Caspian crosses.

In addition to having excellent conformation and producing first class stock, the pure bred Caspian stallion, Hopstone Atesh (Karoun x Khorshid Kola*), is, himself, an outstanding performer. Ridden by Ana Rattray, he has competed successfully in jumping competitions against open horses and won the stallion class at Warkworth Show for several years running.

Atesh has sired a strong field of competition and show horses in New Zealand for which he was awarded the Progeny Award for Show Hunter ponies in 1997.

Using Helen Rattrays Anglo-Arab mare Arabelle, they produced some outstanding performance stock, Cheleken Mikado, Cheleken Titus and Cheleken Victoriana. The latter was a confidence giving pony, capable of carrying an inexperienced rider safely over a small course. At her first show she won five firsts, one second and a Reserve Championship. At her second show she took two firsts, one second and a Reserve Championship. Her third show gained her five firsts. To illustrate the sort of company that she was capable of standing in, she was third in the Championship behind the eventual Supreme Champion Pony at the Royal Show, which also became Champion Pony of the Year.

Mikado was also highly successful. In 1984, as a four year old, he was 13.2 Show Jumper of the Year at the New Zealand Horse of the Year Show against the cream of New Zealand's show jumping ponies. He was Champion Hunter at four shows and out of two starts was first and second in pony racing events at Kiawaka and Ellerslie. His racing wins totalled $1,000. The success of this line continued with Arabelle's 'grandchildren' Cheleken Arzanna and Cheleken Thistledown.

Probably the most successful of Atesh's sons is Cheleken Xerxes, a 14.1 chestnut gelding out of a thoroughbred mare. Xerxes proved to be an outstandingly versatile and successful pony who was at stud for several years before being gelded and starting a very worthwhile competitive career. His progeny all have the good temperament and outstanding scopey jump of the Caspian. Xerxes was an Open Show Hunter, qualifying for the Horse of the Year Show in New Zealand twice, an Open Eventer and a Grade C Show Jumper.

Cheleken Flashback, a 16.0 hands quarter bred Caspian by Xerxes was placed in Novice Horse Trials, Dressage and Show Hunter classes. He was then very successfully competed by a young competition rider in Northland and his placings included fourth in the New Zealand Three Day Event.

Cheleken Impeccable, by a TB stallion, out of a half bred mare (x Hopstone Atesh) was many times champion and supreme champion on the flat and has now been sold to South Island where she has beaten many established and well known riding ponies.

Cheleken Playboy, a 14.1 half bred gelding (Hopstone Atesh x TB) has many placings in show jumping and eventing and has also qualified for the Horse of the Year Show.

Other notable performers include Cheleken Phantom a Grade A Show Jumper (sold to Japan early in 1994), and Cheleken Lord and Master, a quarter bred Show Hunter Champion/ Eventer.

Most of the ponies were schooled at home by Ana Rattray and her sister until above-novice standard on the flat and over fences, followed by a season doing show hunter classes, show jumping/eventing before being placed on the market. All perform well for their new owners and are building up a reputation in New Zealand for the Caspian cross as versatile and talented horses and ponies.

WESTERN AUSTRALIA

Pure bred Caspian stallion, Hopstone Kaftar, bred in the UK (Mehran x Taliyeh) and exported to Western Australia by Mr. & Mrs. Gyles of Jarrahdale, amazed audiences with his temperament in a Caspian Display Team, which included everything from dressage to tent-pegging at full gallop, and fire-jumping. Following a back injury, Kaftar was broken to harness, where he is equally successful.

SOUTH AUSTRALIA

Caspian classes have been held annually at the Royal Adelaide Show. In 1984, the Adelaide Advertiser produced a special Caspian supplement after the show which included a spectacular picture of a Caspian, captioned "Jumping like a Thoroughbred". In 1993 Marida Tarikh, bred by the Marida Stud took first place in the mare or filly class. (See Chapter 4 - Marida

Prrester John - Welsh Cob x Caspian by Karoun (bred by Muriel Harris) also driven with
a team of Welsh Cobs as a four-in-hand.

New Zealand - Cheleken Lord and Master - Show Hunter Champion/Eventer - bred by Helen Rattray
- ridden by Ana Rattray (out of an Anglo Arab mare: sire by Hopstone Atesh x tb mare)
(Courtesy of Barbara Thomson)

Stud). Kurt Wehner 's Marida Hadi was a regular winner in harness and Marshall Steer's part bred, Tori Lady, took part in trotting races, driven by children under twelve.

80C3

CHAPTER TEN
THE PRESENT DAY AND FUTURE POSITION OF THE CASPIAN

Building up a sound breeding base has been a slow and sometimes floundering process. The slow growth rate in the early days was due to the abysmally small numbers in existence. The problem which breeders faced was how to produce sufficient stock to meet a growing market for showing and performance stock, whilst maintaining sufficient stock for breeding, with the correct balance of bloodlines.

Buyers wishing to purchase Caspians had to travel long distances in order to see small numbers or even individual animals. Often, they would choose one, for performance, which the breeder was unable to release because of the rarity of the line or a unique characteristic. The long waiting list, and lack of classes in which potential buyers could exhibit, soon gave way to impatience and the potential market looked elsewhere.

The growth in numbers has now released stock from sole breeding duties; therefore an increasing number of mares now compete successfully.

There is little doubt that interest from the American market and, more recently, from Scandinavia, has spurred the breeding programmes of UK and Australasian breeders.

Caspians Registered prior to 1998
At the end of 1997, 770 Caspian births (or foundation stock) had been registered with the International Caspian Stud Book.

432	UK
93	SOUTH AUSTRALIA
50	WESTERN AUSTRALIA
28	NZ
124	IRAN
27	USA

232 foundation stock and foals were registered with the Iranian Society between their rediscovery in 1965 and the end of 1997. However, over 100 of these were 'wiped out' during the Revolution and the Iran/Iraq war and are not included in the current International Stud Book.

The sales to America boosted the number of mares covered in the UK in 1995 and a record number of mares foaled in 1996 and 1997. The first USA foal was born in 1995.

It is uncertain how many registered Caspians are still alive, as the Societies have lost touch with a number of registered stock, including the Bermudan gelding, Darius, but it is unlikely that they number more than 550. Of these, approximately 200 are used primarily for performance or are too old for breeding, leaving a total of approximately 350 breeding mares and stallions worldwide. At the beginning of 1998, there were 23 licensed stallions standing at public stud in the UK. The death of Forstals Barewa and the export of Henden Khodee to Norway, and Henden Zebedee and Forstals Danda Daniska to the USA, brought this number down to 19.

From these numbers it is obvious that there is no room for complacency.

Some of the founder lines are thin, mainly female, but, although efforts need to be concentrated upon strengthening these lines, none have yet been totally lost. Of the original pre-revolution imports to the UK, the mares, Shirine*, Siyah Gosh* and Pari* are still alive.

The way forward

Competition seems to be the way forward in proving the true value of the pure bred and cross bred Caspian.

The Caspian/Arabian/Thoroughbred cross should result in the production of the type of quality performance animal produced in New Zealand, whilst crossing with native ponies will produce performance stock such as Prester John and "Charlie and Chester" bred by Rosemary and Muriel Harris.

There is a still a need to expel the myth that the Caspian is a 'miniature', with nothing to offer to the world of riding and competition. The word 'miniature', so often used to describe the Caspian, has caused them to become confused with the "toy horse" and the "Falabella".

Owners need to be selective about which classes in which to enter their own 'type' of pure bred Caspian. The sort of controversy which surrounds the Welsh Section B pony also affects the Caspian: 'If it is a mountain pony, how can it be a show pony? If it is a show pony, how can it be a mountain pony?'

Following the blood-typing of Caspians in 1990 at Kentucky University (and prior to the importation of the 1994 shipment of Caspians from Iran to the UK) Gus Cothran stated that:

"As would be expected, there is an overall positive inbreeding level for the breed, which would lead to reduced genetic variation, but the inbreeding is not high. In addition, there has been no increase in inbreeding levels in the last six years, up to the 1990 crop of foals.

Finally, founder genetic contributions to the current population and the proportion of the remaining founder geome at risk of loss were estimated by pedigree analysis. In order to maximize the conservation of genetic variation in a closed population, such as the English Caspians, it is important to even up the genetic contribution of the founders. Six of the 20 founders account for 53.1% of the current genetic variation. The remaining 14 founders (including Jehan, exported to USA, whose pure-bred offspring - a single unused stallion - died in the Iranian Revolution) contribute from 6.7% to less than 1% to the genetic make-up of the current population. The founders with a disproportionately high contribution are Ostad*, Ruba*, Jehan Afrouz*, Daria Nour*, Mitra* and Khorshid Kola* in order of % contribution.

The founders with the lowest contribution (in order of lowest contribution) are Felfel*, Anahita*, Alamara*, Taloche*, Shirine* and Fatemeh*. Special efforts should be made to increase the genetic contribution of these six founders in order to help preserve genetic variation within the breed. This means that offspring or descendants of these horses should be preferentially bred, especially compared to the six founders with the highest genetic contribution. In some cases, this may be difficult or undesirable.

The judgment of both the breeders and the registry must be exercised to determine how much evening of genetic contribution can/or should be accomplished. To date, the breeding strategy for the Caspians has been quite good. Continued intelligent breeding practices should maintain genetic variation within the Caspian Pony breed in England".

E. Gus Cothran, Kentucky University

Since the above was written, the order of weakness has altered slightly and the foundation female Fatemeh* is currently the weakest bloodline in existence outside Iran.

Lowest contributing foundation bloodlines:

Felfel* is represented only through the offspring of the mare Hopstone Banafsheh. Two sons now stand at srud. Banafsheh also has several daughters, being regularly bred. The line is strong through outcross breeding with Forstals Barewa, and Runnymede Orion, from this line, has bred several daughters.

Anahita* via

Pourandokht representation is sparse through the offspring of the mare Touran. Although she bred nine foals, only one, Hopstone Khandeh, is still available for breeding. A Touran daughter, Hopstone Qahve, bred three foals in NZ. Her stallion son, Sunbeam Tarminh died in 1995. He was relatively isolated on Anglesey (North Wales) and never covered a Caspian mare. Out of twelve second generation stock only two grand-daughters remain in the UK., Eastern Jamuna, also regularly ridden and shown successfully, and Miran Khala. Touran has one granddaughter in NZ and a grandson and granddaughter in the USA. Pourandokht is now represented by one of the 1994 imports.

Alamara* is represented only through Momtaz-e-Mahal. Her daughters, Every Roshana (Henden Stud) and Every Lara (NZ) have been regularly bred. Her daughter, Vashta, is represented only through the stallion Middleton Shir, unused until 1996.

Taloche* Her daughter Hopstone Lili, is now in France. The line in the UK now depends on one daughter, Chestnuts Soraya, and a small number of stock sired by Hopstone Xerxes. A grandson of Lili has recently been exported to Tina Staples of Connecticut, USA.

Shirine* is represented only through her daughters, Hopstone Asal, Hopstone Spark Ariana and Spark Shirine Shara; also through the stallion, Spark Shiraz, standing in 1999 and 2000 with Bytham Stud, Lincolnshire. Ariana, who has bred only two daughters, is now in Connecticut and in foal to the grandson of Lili, mentioned above. This line is now being concentrated upon by breeders and Spark Tabriz, a son of Spark Shirine Shara, has been exported to Texas to ensure continuation of the line in the USA.

Fatemeh* is now the most threatened of the foundation lines. Her only daughter still available for breeding is Kineton Kodam. Two other daughters are sadly unavailable for breeding. Kodam has bred several colts but the line still remains sparse and needs to be concentrated upon. One of her sons will stand at stud in the UK from 1999 and Hopstone Bahar, a grand-daughter of Fatemeh* has bred a filly foal to Persicus Amir, in Norway.

Kentucky University - Recent Findings

Relationship of the Caspian to other horse breeds

At the request of the author, Gus Cothran agreed to document the results of his research regarding the relationship of the Caspian to many other horse breeds around the world. As some of his work is too detailed for this book, sections have been omitted. However, despite the technical nature of the work, it is felt necessary to include most of it in order to illustrate the probable relationship between the Caspian and the Arab.

"Much of the interest in the Caspian horse has to do with its presumed age as a breed and its possible ancestral relationship to the modern Arabian horse. Much has been written about the evidence for the antiquity of the Caspian elsewhere in this volume. What I will address here is the question of the relationship of the Caspian to other horse breeds and particularly those horses classified as Arabian. Genetic relationships can be tested using genetic markers based upon blood group and biochemical variations. Genetic markers are inherited characteristics that occur in more than one form (genetic variants). The basic premise is that the more genetic markers that are shared between two organisms or groups of organisms, the more closely related they are. Genetic markers and genetic relationship estimates based upon these markers also can be analysed to develop hypotheses of ancestry."

".....The individual genetic units analysed are called loci or systems. The different forms that can occur at these loci are termed alleles or variants. At each locus an individual has two copies of the gene (one inherited from the father and one from the mother). If the two forms of the gene are the same the individual is homozygous and if they are different the term is heterozygous. The percentage of times each allele of a gene occurs in a population is the allele or gene frequency. The basis for most of the analyses are the allele frequencies."

".... the information to interpret becomes very large very quickly. Most commonly these results are expressed as branching diagrams known as trees or dendograms."

"....The genetic analyses of the Caspian to other domestic horse breeds is based upon data from 17 genetic systems. Seven systems were blood group loci while the remaining 10 were biochemical loci. For the purpose of this analysis a total of 125 genetic variants were recognised....."

"Before going into the analysis, there are several things that must be kept in mind. First, all horses are descended from a common ancestor and thus share alleles at all the genetic systems analyses for this study. In general, domestic horse breeds differ in the assortment of genetic variants found within the breed and frequency of variants. Certain variants are much more likely to be found within particular breed types than within others (for example, draft horses versus Arabian type horses). The second point is that horses have been cross bred to a very large extent over the history of the species under domestication. This means that no matter what the distinctiveness of the races of horses that formed the basis of domestic horses was, this distinctiveness has been obscured by interbreeding. Another point that must be kept in mind is the demographic history of the breed. Small population size, inbreeding or a dominant stallion can cause random changes in gene frequencies or the loss of alleles. Such changes also can mask relationships when determination of relationships must be based upon altered gene frequencies... The main point is that when dealing with closely related breeds with such diverse histories, accessing genetic relationship based upon genetic markers that represent a very small part of the genome can be difficult."

"Despite the above potential difficulties, in general gene marker analysis of horse breeds gives very reasonable dendograms based upon what is known historically. There are six major branches (or groupings) of the horse tree based upon my analyses to date. The most distinctive clusters are the draft horse breeds and the northern European pony breeds. To some extent these could represent a single major branch rather than two. The other major groupings are Oriental breeds, Thoroughbred related breeds, gaited North American breeds, and Iberian peninsula derived breeds. These major groupings are consistent across all analyses and therefore appear to represent major genetic units. Of course, it must be remembered that this is just based upon the breeds that have been tested and additional groupings may become apparent if more breeds, particularly ones from geographical areas such as Eastern Asia, are tested. In addition, there are breeds that do not clearly fit into any of these groupings or do not fit into the cluster where they might be expected based upon physical appearance. ..."

"Two sets of Caspians have been analysed. The first group was 53 horses sampled from the population in England. The second group was of 41 Caspians from Iran. Although there were some genetic marker differences between the two samples, these were minor and could have represented sampling errors, they clearly were related and represented a single breed. For this reason the pooled sample of 94 individuals also was analysed."

"A number of different genetic similarity or distance measures were calculated for each of the three Caspian samples with about 80 domestic horse breeds. For the purposes of this report, only 66 of these breeds will be considered. Each of the 66 fits into one of the six major groups described above. All genetic resemblance measures gave essentially the same results so I will only discuss the genetic similarity calculated using Roger's 1972 coefficient S as this measure provides reasonably good discrimination between closely related groups. It also is easily interpreted; a value for S of 1.0 means the two populations have identical gene frequencies at all tested loci while a value of S of 0.0 means they are completely different. In comparisons of horse breeds, S generally ranges between 0.5 and 0.95."

"For English, Iranian and combined samples of Caspians mean S for each of the horse groupings was calculated. For the English Caspian population, highest mean S was with Iberian descent (.809) followed by that with ponies (.804) and Arabian breeds (.795). These values are fairly low which usually is due to low overall genetic diversity. However, the level of genetic variation in the English Caspian is very close to the average for domestic horse breeds so this is not the answer. A more likely reason for the low S values is an unusual combination of alleles related to the small number of individuals that founded the population.

The Iranian Caspian population had the highest mean S with the Arabian breeds (.859) followed by ponies (.855) and Iberian breeds (832). These values are more like what is commonly seen with all mean values above .80. The S values for the combined sample of Caspians was highest with Arabian breeds (.855) followed by Iberian breeds (.842) and ponies (.835). **Thus, overall, Caspians showed highest similarity with Arabian type breeds**. Next closest were the breeds with Iberian peninsula origins followed by pony breeds."

"Cluster analysis strongly supports the primary association of the Caspian with the Arabian breeds. "

Tree No. 1:

(A portion of a dendogram of an analysis of 56 horse breeds. Draft horse and pony breeds not shown)

"........ The Oriental type horses form a distinct cluster in the centre of Tree 1, The only exception is the Moroccan Barb which fits in the middle of the cluster of Iberian horse breeds. Within the Oriental cluster those breeds which are true Arabian breeds form a tight group with the Kurd and Akhal-Teke on the outside of this cluster. The Caspian data here is the combined English and Iranian data. The Caspian is the base breed in a subcluster that also includes the Yabou (a native Iranian breed from the same general area as that where the Caspian was found) and the Turkoman (closely related to the Akhal -Teke). This group represents the most primitive (ancestral) breeds of the Oriental cluster and **the Caspian has the most primitive position of these three breeds."**

Tree No. 2:

(This tree utilizes gene frequencies from the Oriental breeds and mean gene frequencies from the other major breed groups).

"Data from the Przewalski horse was used to root the tree. Again, the Oriental breeds form a distinct cluster and **the two Caspian populations occupy the ancestral position within this cluster.** The relative position of the Arabian cluster to the other major breed groups is similar to that in Tree 1."

Tree No. 3:

(Only the Oriental and Iberian horse breeds are shown here)

"The Oriental cluster is similar to that in Tree 1 with the exception that the Moroccan Barb is positioned within the Arabian cluster rather than the Iberian cluster. The Caspian, Yabou, Turkoman cluster occurs as in Tree 1 with the exception that this is the English Caspian population rather than pooled Caspian data. **The Iranian Caspian population occupies the most primitive position of the Arab and Iberian breeds.** This is consistent with the high genetic similarity of the Caspian to Iberian breeds."

Tree No. 4:

(Relates only to Oriental breeds)

"Again the true Arabian breeds cluster in the centre of the tree. These breeds are flanked by the Kurd, Akhal-Teke and Moroccan Barb. The Iranian Caspian forms the base of this cluster. The English sample of Caspians occupies the base (or ancestral) position of the entire tree."

The various methods and groupings of breeds give very similar trees overall. This consistency is grounds for accepting these results at face value; however, other things must be considered in interpretation of these results."

"Based upon geography and physical conformation, the Caspian would be predicted to be an Oriental type of horse genetically and this was the case. Based upon physical conformation, the Caspian looks more like the true Arabian breeds, however, genetically it is more like the other Oriental breeds such as the Turkoman. This result is consistent with geographical distribution. Archeological evidence suggests that a horse very similar to the Caspian has existed in this region for over 3000 years. The genetic results are not inconsistent with this hypothesis but do not provide conclusive information. The phylogenetic analysis suggest that the Caspian could be primitive for the Oriental type horse analysed. However, this is not proof of an ancestral relationship. A number of factors (such as crossbreeding, inbreeding or sampling errors) could result in an ancestral position on a phylogenetic tree. In the case of the Caspian, inbreeding and sampling errors do not appear to be likely factors. Crossbreeding of the Caspian to other Oriental type breeds has almost certainly happened, however, the amount of crossing within recent times does not appear to be great. This observation is based upon the consistency of genetic types across the Caspian horses tested and the size of the Caspian. Although single genes can effect body size (dwarfism) it is not likely that all Caspians are homozygous for a recessive gene that controls body size (if there was a single dominant gene larger horses should occasionally be produced). This is not consistent with the level of genetic variation in Caspians."

"In examining the question of relationship of the Caspian to other horse breeds, the relatively close relationship of the Caspian to horses of the Iberian peninsula must be considered. Based upon geographical and historical considerations, there is no doubt that there has been cross breeding of Iberian and Oriental horses. The questions are to what degree, how long ago and in which direction. In prehistoric times it is likely that horses of Northern Africa and Europe interbred in the area of the current Iberian peninsula. This is consistent with the genetic data. Since the domestication of the horse, there has been exchange of horses in both directions."

"The Caspian is unlikely to have been directly involved in the genetic exchange among Oriental and Iberian horses. However, two individuals of Caspians from Iran carried the Pi-W allele which is primarily associated with Iberian derived horse breeds. The Pi-W variant also has been observed in the Moroccan Barb but in no other Oriental horses to date. The significance of this observation cannot presently be evaluated as there are many possible ways this distribution of the Pi-W variant could have occurred. However this Pi variant is only a small part of the high similarity of the Caspian to horses of the Iberian peninsula. **This overall high similarity again suggests a primitive position for the Caspian in relation to other Oriental and Iberian horse breeds.**"

"In conclusion, the genetic evidence is consistent with the Caspian horse as being ancestral to modern Oriental horses. However, this evidence cannot be considered to be proof that the Caspian is the ancestor to modern Arabian type breeds. As discussed earlier, there are other factors which could influence genetic similarity and the phylogenetic trees. Also, the phylogenetic trees should be treated as hypotheses that must be investigated further. Future analyses will include data from mitochondrial and nuclear DNA. "

"Regardless of the outcome of future research, the Caspian is a unique breed of horse that deserves the efforts directed at its preservation."

ೞೞ

TREE 1

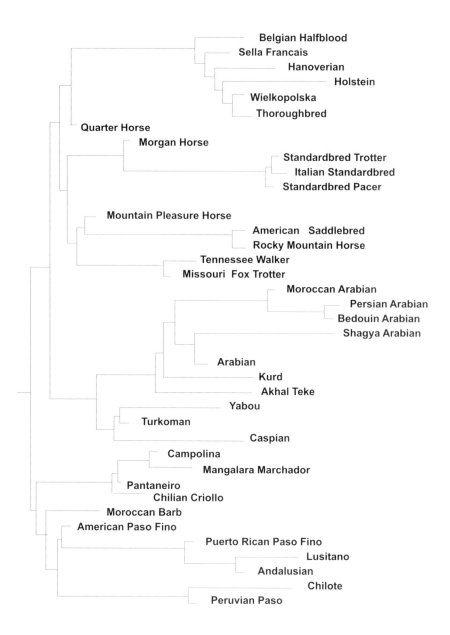

TREE 2

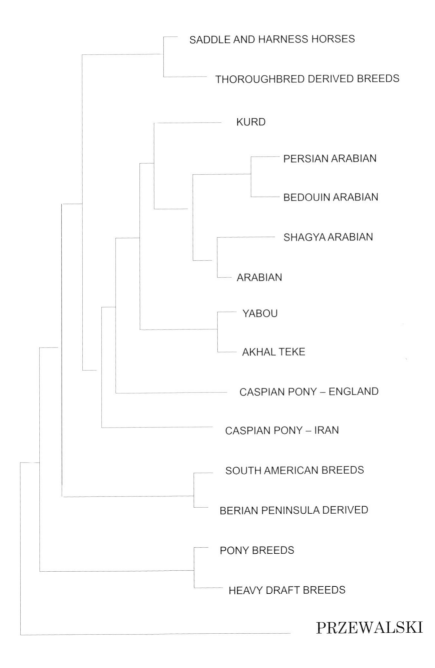

SADDLE AND HARNESS HORSES

THOROUGHBRED DERIVED BREEDS

KURD

PERSIAN ARABIAN

BEDOUIN ARABIAN

SHAGYA ARABIAN

ARABIAN

YABOU

AKHAL TEKE

CASPIAN PONY – ENGLAND

CASPIAN PONY – IRAN

SOUTH AMERICAN BREEDS

BERIAN PENINSULA DERIVED

PONY BREEDS

HEAVY DRAFT BREEDS

PRZEWALSKI

TREE 3

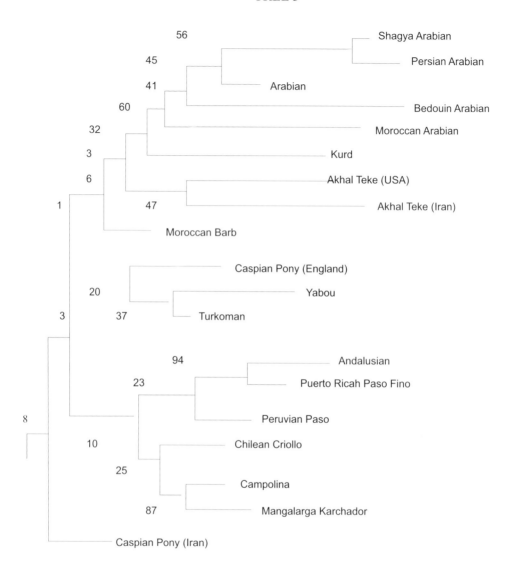

TREE 4

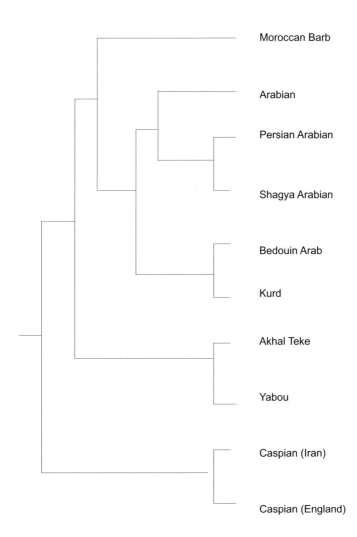

Cheleken Xerxes, shown as a yearling colt - New Zealand. A son of Hopstone Atesh out of a Thoroughbred mare, Xerxes sired top quality threequarter-bred show hunter ponies.

Hopstone Jamshyd - (Palang* x Hopstone Zara) owned by Jennifer Quinney. A former Breed Champion, Jamshyd has been well placed in driving classes at major shows and has competed extensively and successfully under saddle.

CHRONOLOGY

3000 BC	Evidence of existence of Caspian type horses from this date
500 BC	Horses of Caspian type depicted on seal of King Darius the Great
1965	Caspian stallion, Ostad*, found in Amol, Iran
1966	Jehan*(S) exported to Great Falls, Virginia, USA
1970	Joan Taplin exported Mitra*(M), Momtaz-e-Mahal(M), Daria Nour*(S) to Bermuda
1971	Khorshid Kola*(M) and Rostam(S) presented to H.R.H. Prince Philip, UK
1972	Atesheh born in Hungary en route to the UK
1972	Amu Daria and Roshan arrive in UK from Bermuda (Mrs. Mary Niebel)
1972	Stud formed in UK with Amu Daria and Roshan and loan of stock from H.R.H. Prince Philip.
1973	Formation of the Royal Horse Society, Iran
1973	Herd of 23 Caspians purchased by the Royal Horse Society
1974	Sale of Norouzabad Equestrian Centre
1974	Caspian stallion, Ruba II, was Supreme Ch. Pony at Salon Du Cheval, Paris.
1974	Export of Mehregan(M) to USA
1974	Shipment of Stock from Iran to UK Taliyeh(M) Karoun(S) Maroun(S) Mehran(S)
1975	Export of Nourie*(M) to Venezuala, USA
1975	Shipment of Stock from Iran to UK Susiana(M) Gulpar(M)Aloucheh(M)Touran (M) Purchase of Ruba II and export to Australia via UK
1975	Export of stock to Australia Susiana(M)Gulpar(M)Aloucheh(M)
1975	The Firouz family move to Turkoman Steppes
1976	Purchase of remaining stock from Bermuda by Caspian Stud UK Gift of Momtaz-e-Mahal(M) to H.R.H. Prince Philip
1976	Herd numbered 20 mares and 3 stallions
1976	Wolf attack on herd in Iran
1976	Emergency evacuation of six mares and one stallion to UK Pari*(M), Fatemeh*(M), Shirine*(M), Siyah Gosh*(M), Doueez*(M), Taloche*(M), Palang*(S) (a seventh mare, Abrisham, was discarded - as possibly not Caspian).
1977	Remainder of herd confiscated by Royal Horse Society
1978	Shipment of stock to Australia/New Zealand
1978	Start of Revolution in Iran
1979	Departure of the Shah to USA - 16th January Caspians auctioned off by the Revolutionary Guard Ban from keeping more than one horse in Iran
1980	Iran/Iraq war
1981	Death of Charles Jenvey
1981	Firouz family move to Kurdan
1986	Three mares and a stallion purchased from horse dealers
1987	Fereshteh - first Caspian born in Iran following ban on keeping horses

1987	Alvand(S) from old Royal Horse Society loaned to Louise Firouz
1987	Death of Arthur Griffin (partner Caspian Stud UK)
1989	Death of the imported mare Touran and foundation stallion Palang*
1989	Six Caspians found amongst horses from Iran/Iraq war effort.
1990	Research begun by Gus Cothran at Kentucky University
1990	Death of imported mares, Taliyeh and Momtaz-e-Mahal
1992	Death of imported stallion, Karoun
1993	Death of the stallion Jehan* (first Caspian to be exported from Iran/ USA)
	Death of HRH Prince Philip's stallion Rostam
1993	Export of three mares and four stallions from Iran to UK
	through wartorn southern Russia
1994	Arrival of above in UK
	Ai Banou(M) Kouchek Khan(S) Khoshgel Khanum(M)
	Amir(S) Yussef(S) Tehou(M) Nicky(S) Prefix: Persicus
1994	Persicus Amir and Persicus Tehou exported to Belgium
1994	Death of Narcy Firouz
1994	Death of imported stallion, Mehran, and mare, Atesheh
1994	Sale of stock from UK to U.S.A.
1995	Further shipments of stock from UK to U.S.A.
	Shipment of stock from South Australia to U.S.A.
	Shipment of stock from New Zealand to U.S.A.
	Shipment of stock from Western Australia to U.S.A.
1995	Sale of stock from Persicus Stud in Iran to Ministry of Jehad
1995	Involvement of John Schneider-Merck in the search for, and funding of, foundation stock in Iran
1995	Death of imported stallion, Maroun
1996	Death of Iranian mare Gulpar (Australia)
1998	Death of Forstals Barewa
1998	First imports to Norway and Sweden
1999	11/12th September - First International Conference held in Texas
2000	Death of Shirine
2003	Exports to Holland and Germany
2004	11/12/13th August - Second International Caspian Conference in Rutland, England
2004	Death of Amu Daria
2004	Export of new bloodlines to Australia, Zarin Taze Majara (S), Henden Balut (gelding) Spark Zarrin Tara (M), Spark Persia (M), Sirhowy Arziz (M)
2005	At December 2005 – 1,500 Caspians registered in the ICSB

* Foundation stock
(S) Stallion
(M) Mare

BREED TYPE AND STANDARD

GENERAL

The Caspian is a horse, not a pony, and therefore should be viewed in the same manner as when judging a Thoroughbred, i.e. the limbs, body and head should all be in proportion to each other. Foreshortened limbs or a head out of proportion are faults. The overall impression should be of a well-bred, elegant horse in miniature.

EYES: Almond shape, large, dark, set low, often prominent.
NOSTRILS: Large, low set, finely chiselled, capable of considerable dilation during action.
EARS: Short, wide apart, alert, finely drawn, often noticeably in-pricked at the tips.

HEAD: Wide, vaulted forehead (in most cases the parietal bones do not form a crest but remain open to the occipital crest). Frontal bone should blend into nasal bone in a pleasing slope. Very deep, prominent cheek bones and great width between cheekbones where they join at throat. Head tapers to a fine, firm muzzle.
NECK: Long, supple neck with a finely modelled throat latch.

SHOULDERS AND WITHERS: Long, sloping, well modelled, with good wither.
BODY: Characteristically slim with deep girth. Chest width in proportion to width of body - it is a fault to have 'both legs out of the same hole'. Close-coupled, with well-defined hindquarters and good 'saddle space'.

QUARTERS: Long and sloping from hip to point of buttocks. Great length from stifle to hock.
HOCKS: Owing to their mountain origin Caspians may have more angled hock than lowland breeds.

LIMBS: Characteristically slender with dense, flat bone and flat knees. Good slope to pasterns, neither upright nor over-sloping.

HOOF: Both front and back are oval and neat, with immensely strong wall and sole, and very little frog.

COAT, SKIN AND HAIR: Skin thin, fine and supple, dark except under white markings. Coat silky and flat, often with iridescent sheen in summer. Thick winter coat. Mane and tail abundant but fine and silky. Mane usually lies flat (as in Thoroughbreds) but can grow to great lengths. Tail carried gaily in action. Limbs generally clean with little or no feathering at the fetlock.

COLOURS: All colours, except piebald or skewbald (pinto). Greys will go through many shades of roan before fading to near white at maturity.

HEIGHT: Varies with feeding, care and climate. Recorded specimens have ranged from under 10 hands to over 13 hands. Growth rate in the young is extremely rapid with the young Caspian making most of its height in the first 18 months, filling out with maturity.

ACTION/ PERFORM- ANCE: Natural floating action at all gaits. Long, low swinging trot with spectacular use of the shoulder. Smooth, rocking canter, rapid flat gallop. Naturally light and agile with exceptional jumping ability.

TEMPERAMENT: Highly intelligent and alert, but very kind and willing.

109

BIBLIOGRAPHY

The Caspian Miniature Horse of Iran	Firouz, Louise	Field Research Projects 1972
Osteological and Historical Implications of the Caspian Miniature Horse to Early Horse Domestication in Iran	Firouz, Louise The Royal Horse Society of Iran	Hungarian Academy of Sciences
Horses - their role in the History of Man	Hartley Edwards, Elwyn	Willow Books 1987
Pony Magazine	Firouz, Louise	Dec. 1968
The Horse of the Desert	Brown, W.R.	New York 1948
Geographical Journal	Noel	1921
The Horse through Fifty Centuries of Civilization	Dent, Anthony	Phaidon 1974
International Caspian Stud Book Vol. 111	Alderson, Elizabeth Alderson, Lawrence	Countrywide Livestock Ltd. 1983
Riding Through My Life	HRH Princess Ann with Ivor Herbert	Pelham 1991
Curzon's Persia	Curzon G.N.	Sidgewick & Jackson
The Ark	Alderson, Lawrence	Rare Breeds Survival Trust
Riding Magazine	Spooner, Glenda	
Horsemen of the Steppes	Walter Fairservis	Brockhampton Press Ltd.

Eastern Jamal - bred by Jennifer Quinney, UK, and purchased by ProtoArabians, USA photo: Stine

❧ EPILOGUE ❧

That the Caspian has survived is due to the dedication of a handful of people who have thrown themselves, and usually their families, heart and soul into what has sometimes seemed an impossible dream. Without the resilience shown by horses and owners alike, the breed would undoubtedly have perished.

There have been times when the problems have seemed insurmountable and the costs too high, financially, physically and psychologically. Despite the hardships, Caspian owners are proud to have been at the start of a modern day adventure involving a unique horse, which has, in all probability, played a major role in the history of the majority of hot-blooded breeds in existence today.

The Ministry of Jehad, in Iran, has accepted the importance of the Caspian horse as a National Treasure and have taken a responsible role in the preservation of the breed in its natural home.

American interest has spurred breeding to numbers which should ensure the continuation of the breed.

But for the stubborn persistence of Louise Firouz, and the offer, all those years ago, of sanctuary for some of her Caspians from H.R.H. Prince Philip, the Caspian may still remain hidden behind the mountain peaks of the Alborz range in Northern Iran. His Royal Highness could not then have foreseen the gravity of his advice. In little more than thirty years much research has been instigated and much learned about this fascinating breed. No doubt the research - and the controversy - will continue for many years to come.

❧

INDEX